A Rulebook for Arguments

Fifth Edition

Anthony Weston

A Rulebook for Arguments

Fifth Edition

Hackett Publishing Company, Inc.
Indianapolis/Cambridge

For further information, please address
Hackett Publishing Company, Inc.
P.O. Box 44937
Indianapolis, Indiana 46244-0937

www.hackettpublishing.com

Cover art and interior design by Elizabeth L. Wilson
Composition by Integrated Composition Systems

Library of Congress Cataloging-in-Publication Data

Names: Weston, Anthony, 1954– author.
Title: A rulebook for arguments / Anthony Weston.
Description: Fifth edition. | Indianapolis ; Cambridge : Hackett Publishing
   Company, Inc., 2017. | Includes bibliographical references.
Identifiers: LCCN 2017027845 | ISBN 9781624666544 (pbk.) |
   ISBN 9781624666872 (cloth)
Subjects: LCSH: Reasoning. | Logic. | English language—Rhetoric.
Classification: LCC BC177 .W47 2017 | DDC 168—dc23
LC record available at https://lccn.loc.gov/2017027845

The paper used in this publication meets the minimum requirements of
American National Standard for Information Sciences—Permanence of
Paper for Printed Library Materials, ANSI Z39.48–1984.
∞

Contents

Preface

This book is a brief introduction to the art of making arguments. It sticks to the bare essentials. I have found that students and writers often need just such a list of reminders and rules, not lengthy introductory explanations. This book is therefore organized around specific rules, illustrated and explained soundly but above all briefly. It is not a textbook but a *rule*book.

Instructors too, I have found, often wish to assign such a rulebook, a treatment that students can consult and understand on their own and that therefore does not claim too much class time. Here again, it is important to be brief—the point is to help students get on with their actual arguments—but the rules must be stated with enough substance that an instructor can simply refer a student to Rule 6 or Rule 16 rather than give an entire explanation each time it is needed. Brief but self-sufficient—that is the fine line I have tried to follow.

This rulebook also can be used in a course that gives critical attention to arguments. It will need to be supplemented with exercises and more examples, but many texts are already available that consist largely or wholly of such exercises and examples. *Those* texts, however, also need to be supplemented—with what this rulebook offers: simple rules for putting good arguments together. We do not want our students to come out of critical thinking courses knowing only how to shoot down (or just *at*) selected fallacies. Critical thinking can be practiced in a far more constructive spirit. This book is one attempt to suggest how.

Note to the Fifth Edition

Rulebook continues to find a wide use in a variety of schools, from high school to law school, and in other settings too. The world continues to change as well. In this fifth edition there are several corresponding changes. Most notably, I have added a new final chapter, "Public Debates," which repositions a few of the old rules but mostly adds new ones. The state of our public debate at the moment is pretty sorry, and while this surely has many causes, a better understanding of the etiquette and the ethics of good public debate should help. Six short rules—but what a difference they might make!

Smaller changes include a number of updated examples, drawing on a wider and more contemporary range of sources. Goodbye Einstein, hello Beyoncé. This edition is a little fresher, a little tighter, a bit more humorous. Some of the rules have acquired punchy subtitles. This is no time to be timid about the need for good arguments and better ways of arguing, either, so you may find this new edition somewhat edgier as well.

For instructors and students who may be interested, I am happy to add that a companion textbook to *A Rulebook for Arguments* is now available. David Morrow and I have written it ourselves: *A Workbook for Arguments*. *Workbook* includes the entire *Rulebook*, but between each section of this brief guide, *Workbook* interpolates further explanations and extensive examples and exercises, with a thorough selection of sample answers as well. Many thanks to Professor Morrow for convincing me and Hackett Publishing Company of the need for and appeal of such a textbook, and then doing the lion's share of the work on it, carrying it now through two editions (first edition 2013; second edition 2016). David's insights and suggestions have helped shape this new edition of *Rulebook* as well.

Among related changes is that a few of the more challenging examples and themes in previous editions of *Rulebook*, most notably philosopher David Hume's challenges to some of the usual arguments for the existence of God, are migrating to *Workbook*, where they can be treated in more depth. In many ways, *Workbook* is a natural follow-up to *Rulebook*, even if you are not in a class that requires it. We hope you will have a look.

By now it is a long list of colleagues, students, family members, and friends who have contributed thoughts, suggestions, or provocations to this and previous editions of *Rulebook*. This time around I would like to single out Deborah Wilkes, president and publisher, and her colleagues at Hackett Publishing Company, whose stalwart support and gentle encouragement has made both *Rulebook* and *Workbook* continuously enjoyable and superlatively produced projects. My continuing gratitude to you all!

Anthony Weston

July 2017

Introduction

What's the point of arguing?

Many people think that arguing is simply stating their prejudices in a new form. This is why many people also think that arguments are unpleasant and pointless. One dictionary definition for "argument" is "disputation." In this sense we sometimes say that two people "*have* an argument": a verbal fistfight. It happens often enough. But it is not what arguments really are.

In this book, "to give an argument" means to offer a set of reasons or evidence in support of a conclusion. Here an argument is not simply a statement of certain views, and it is not simply a dispute. Arguments are efforts to *support* certain views with reasons. Arguments in this sense are not pointless. In fact, they are essential.

Argument is essential, in the first place, because it is a way of finding out which views are better than others. Not all views are equal. Some conclusions can be supported by good reasons. Others have much weaker support. But often we don't know which are which. We need to give arguments for different conclusions and then assess those arguments to see how strong they really are.

Here argument is a means of *inquiry*. Some philosophers and activists have argued, for instance, that the factory farming of animals for meat causes immense suffering to animals and is therefore unjustified and immoral. Are they right? We can't necessarily tell just by consulting our current opinions. Many issues are involved—we need to examine the arguments. Do we have moral obligations to other species, for instance, or is only human suffering really bad? How well can humans live without meat? Some vegetarians have lived to very old ages. Does this show that vegetarian diets are healthier? Or is it irrelevant when you consider that some nonvegetarians also have lived to very old ages? (You might make some progress by asking whether vegetarians live to old age at a higher *rate*.) Or might healthier people tend to become vegetarians, rather than vice versa? All of these questions need to be considered carefully, and the answers are not clear in advance.

Argument is essential for another reason too. Once we have arrived at a conclusion that is well supported by reasons, we use arguments to explain and defend it. A good argument doesn't merely repeat conclusions. Instead it offers reasons and evidence so that other people can make up their minds for themselves. If you become convinced that we should indeed change the way we raise and use animals, for example, you must use arguments to explain how you arrived at your conclusion. That is how you will convince others: by offering the reasons and evidence that convinced *you*. It is not a mistake to have strong views. The mistake is to have nothing else.

Argument grows on you

Typically we learn to "argue" by *assertion*. That is, we tend to start with our conclusions—our desires or opinions—without a whole lot to back them up. And it works, sometimes, at least when we're very young. What could be better?

Real argument, by contrast, takes time and practice. Marshaling our reasons, proportioning our conclusions to the actual evidence, considering objections, and all the rest—these are acquired skills. We have to grow up a little. We have to put aside our desires and our opinions for a while and actually *think*.

School may help—or not. In courses concerned with teaching ever-larger sets of facts or techniques, students are seldom encouraged to ask the sorts of questions that arguments answer. Sure, our Constitution mandates the Electoral College—that's a fact—but is it still a good idea? (For that matter, was it ever a good idea? What were the reasons for it, anyway?) Sure, many scientists believe that there is life elsewhere in the universe, but why? What's the argument? Reasons can be given for different answers. In the end, ideally, you will not only learn some of those reasons but also learn how to weigh them up—and how to seek out more yourself.

Mostly, again, it takes time and practice. This book can help! Moreover, the practice of argument turns out to have some attractions of its own. Our minds become more flexible, open-ended, and alert. We come to appreciate how much difference our own critical thinking can really make. From everyday family life to politics, science, philosophy, and even religion, arguments are constantly offered to us for our consideration, and we may in turn offer back our own. Think of argument as a way to make your own place within these unfolding, ongoing dialogues. What could be better than *that?*

Outline of this book

This book begins by discussing fairly simple arguments, moving then to extended arguments and their use in essays, oral presentations, and finally to public debates.

Chapters I–VI are about composing and assessing *short* arguments. Short arguments simply offer their reasons and evidence briefly, usually in a few sentences or a paragraph. We begin with short arguments for several reasons. First, they are common: in fact so common that they are part of every day's conversation. Second, longer arguments are usually elaborations of short arguments, or a series of short arguments linked together. If you learn to write and assess short arguments first, then you can extend your skills to longer arguments in essays or presentations.

A third reason for beginning with short arguments is that they are the best illustrations both of the common argument forms and of the typical mistakes in arguments. In longer arguments, it can be harder to pick out the main points—and the main problems. Therefore, although some of the rules may seem obvious when first stated, remember that you have the benefit of a simple example. Other rules are hard enough to appreciate even in short arguments.

Chapter VII guides you into sketching and then elaborating an extended argument, considering objections and alternatives as you do. Chapter VIII guides you from there into writing an argumentative essay. Chapter IX then adds rules specifically about oral presentation, and Chapter X about public debate. Again, all of these chapters depend on Chapters I–VI, since extended arguments like these essentially combine and elaborate the kinds of short arguments that Chapters I–VI discuss. Don't skip ahead to the later chapters, then, even if you come to this book primarily for help writing an essay or doing a presentation. The book is short enough that you can read it through from the beginning, so that when you arrive at those later chapters you will have the tools you need to use them well. Instructors might wish to assign Chapters I–VI early in the term and Chapters VII–X when the time comes for essays and public presentations and debates.

Two appendices close out the book. The first is a listing of fallacies: types of misleading arguments that are so tempting and common, they even have their own names. The second offers three rules for constructing and evaluating definitions. Use them when you need them!

I

Short Arguments
Some General Rules

Arguments begin by marshaling reasons and organizing them in a clear and fair way. Chapter I offers general rules for composing short arguments. Chapters II–VI discuss specific *kinds* of short arguments.

1 Resolve premises and conclusion

The very first step in making an argument is to ask yourself what you are trying to prove. What is your conclusion? Remember that the conclusion is the statement for which you are giving reasons. The statements that give your reasons are your *premises*.

Let's say that you want to persuade your friends (or children, or parents, or . . .) to eat more beans. Probably this does not seem like the world's most promising proposition, or the most important either. But it is a good first illustration—and diet does matter! Let's consider how you might make such an argument.

You have your conclusion: we should eat more beans. That is your belief. But why? What are your *reasons*? You may need to state them for yourself, for clarity first of all, and then to check that they really are *good* reasons. Certainly you have to state good reasons clearly if you expect others to agree or to change how they eat.

So again: What *are* your reasons? One main premise probably is that beans are healthy: higher in fibers and protein and lower in fat and cholesterol than what most people eat now. So, properly supplemented, a diet of more beans could lead to a longer and more active life. You may not want to assume that your friends or family have heard, or really appreciated, this reason before—at least it is useful to be reminded.

To get people motivated, it would be helpful to add another main premise as well. Since beans are often stereotyped as boring, why not also argue that bean dishes actually can be varied and exciting? Give some examples, your own favorite bean dishes maybe: spicy black bean taco fillings, for instance, and hummus (made from garbanzo beans). Now you've got an argument—good solid reasons for a clear conclusion.

Even jokes can be arguments, though the reasons may seem silly.

> Living on earth may be tough, but it includes a free ride around the sun every year.[1]

Getting a free ride around the sun is not the sort of reason you normally expect for bearing up when life gets tough. That's what makes the joke funny. But it is still a reason: an attempt to justify the claim that life isn't quite so bad as it may sometimes seem. It's a funny *argument*.

In Rule 1—*Resolve* premises and conclusion—the word "resolve" has two related meanings. One is to *distinguish* them. Your reasons are different from your conclusion: keep them clearly separate. Getting a free ride around the sun is a distinct idea from bearing up when life gets tough, and it logically comes first. It's a premise. Being better able to bear up might be something that follows. It's a conclusion.

Once you have distinguished your premises and conclusion, be sure that both are claims that you want to *commit to*. This is the other meaning of "resolve." If so, proceed. If not, change them! In any case, being clear to yourself is necessary before you can be clear to anyone else.

This book offers you a ready list of different forms that arguments can take. Use this list to develop your premises. To defend a generalization, for instance, check Chapter II. It will remind you that you need to give a series of examples as premises, and it will tell you what sorts of examples to look for. If your conclusion requires a deductive argument like those explained in Chapter VI, the rules outlined in that chapter will tell you what types of premises you need. You may have to try several different arguments before you find one that works well.

---

1. Anonymous, Cool Funny Quotes, http://coolfunnyquotes.com. Accessed 2/6/17.

2

Unfold your ideas in a natural order

Arguments *move*. Reasons and evidence lead to conclusions. But, like any other form of movement, arguments may be graceful or clumsy, sharp or confused, clean or muddled. You want clarity and efficiency—even grace, if you can manage it.

Take the argument about beans once more. If you were now going to write your argument out, how might you do it? One good way would be this:

> We should eat more beans. One reason is that beans are healthy. They are higher in fibers and protein and lower in fat and cholesterol than what most people eat now. Meanwhile, bean dishes can be quite varied and exciting too. Think of spicy black bean taco fillings or hummus.

Each sentence in this passage prepares the way for the next one, and then the next one steps smoothly up to bat. The argument begins by stating its conclusion. This invites stating premises in turn, and the argument obliges by immediately stating a main premise, and then giving a brief reason for it in turn, explaining why beans are healthy. Then it offers the other main premise and its examples. The argument could be laid out in different ways—for example, the second main premise could be first, and/or the conclusion could be drawn at the end rather than the beginning—but either way, each part is in a good place.

Getting an argument to unfold in this smooth way is an accomplishment, especially as arguments get more detailed and complex. It's not easy to work out the right place for each part—and plenty of wrong places are usually available. For example, suppose we wrote the argument like this instead:

> Think of spicy black bean taco fillings or hummus. Beans are higher in fibers and protein and lower in fat and cholesterol than what most people eat now. Bean dishes can be quite varied and exciting. We should eat more beans. Beans are healthy.

These are the same premises and conclusion, but they are in a different order, and the passage leaves out the signposts and transition words that help readers identify premises and conclusions (such as "one reason is that . . ."). The result is that the argument is totally garbled. The examples for the main premises, like how tasty bean dishes can be, are scattered through the passage rather than cited right next to the statement of those premises. You have to read the passage twice just to be sure what the conclusion is. Don't count on your readers to be so patient.

Expect to rearrange your argument several times to find the most natural order. Again, the rules offered in this book should help. You can use them to figure out not only what kinds of premises you need but also how to arrange them in the best order.

3 Start from reliable premises

No matter how well you argue from premises to conclusion, your conclusion will be weak if your premises are weak.

> Nobody in the world today is really happy. Therefore, it seems that human beings are just not made for happiness. Why should we expect what we can never find?

The premise of this argument is the statement that nobody in the world today is really happy. Sometimes, on certain rainy afternoons or in certain moods, this may almost seem true. But ask yourself if this premise really is plausible. Is *nobody* in the world today really happy? Ever? What about that free ride around the sun every year?

At the very least, this premise needs some serious defense, and very likely it is just not true. This argument cannot show, then, that human beings are not made for happiness or that you or I should not expect to be happy.

Sometimes it is easy to start from reliable premises. You may have well-known examples at hand or reliable sources that are clearly in agreement. Other times it is harder. If you are not sure about the reliability of a premise, you may need to do some research and/or give an argument for the premise itself (see Rule 31 for more on this point). If you find you *cannot* argue adequately for your premise(s), then, of course, you need to try some other premise!

4 Be concrete and concise

Avoid abstract, vague, and general terms. "We hiked for hours in the sun" is a hundred times better than "It was an extended period of laborious exertion." Be concise too. Airy elaboration just loses everyone in a fog of words.

NO:

> Regularly turning in for the night at an hour that precedes the time at which most of your compatriots go to bed, combined with the practice of awakening at an hour that is earlier than the hour at which most others arise, will tend to the acquisition of such desirable personal traits as a resilient physical constitution, a comfortably well-established financial situation, and the sort of intellectual abilities and capacity for sagacious discernment and judgment that tend to be conducive to earning the respect of others.

YES:

> Early to bed and early to rise makes a man healthy, wealthy, and wise.

The "No" version might overdo it just a bit (you think?), but you see the point. Ben Franklin's rhyme and rhythm help too, but the most important thing is that his words are sharp, simple, and few.

5　Build on substance, not overtone

Offer actual reasons; don't just play on the overtones of words.

NO:

Having so disgracefully allowed her once-proud passenger railroads to fade into obscurity, America is honor-bound to restore them now!

This is supposed to be an argument for restoring (more) passenger rail service. But it offers no evidence for this conclusion whatsoever, just some emotionally loaded words—shopworn words, too, like a politician on automatic. Did passenger rail "fade" because of something "America" did or didn't do? What was "disgraceful" about this? Many "once-proud" institutions outlive their times, after all—we're not obliged to restore them all. What does it mean to say America is "honor-bound" to do this? Have promises been made and broken? By whom?

Much can be said for restoring passenger rail, especially in this era when the ecological and economic costs of highways are becoming enormous. The problem is that this argument does not say it. It lets the emotional charge of the words do all the work, and therefore really does no work at all. We're left exactly where we started. Overtones may sometimes persuade even when they shouldn't, of course—but remember, here we are looking for actual, concrete evidence.

Likewise, do not try to make your argument look good by using emotionally loaded words to label the other side. Generally, people advocate a position for serious and sincere reasons. Try to figure out their view—try to understand their *reasons*—even if you disagree entirely. For example, people who question a new technology are probably not in favor of "going back to the caves." (What *are* they in favor of? Maybe you need to ask.) Likewise, a person who believes in evolution is not claiming that her grandparents were monkeys. (And again: what *does* she think?) In general, if you can't imagine how anyone could hold the view you are attacking, you probably just don't understand it yet.

6 Use consistent terms

Short arguments normally have a single theme or thread. They carry one idea through several steps. Therefore, couch that idea in clear and carefully chosen terms, and mark each new step by using those very same terms again.

In their classic composition handbook, *The Elements of Style*, William Strunk and E. B. White cite Jesus's famous Beatitudes as a compelling illustration of what they call "parallel construction" or "expressing coordinate ideas in similar form."

> Blessed are the poor in spirit: for theirs is the kingdom of Heaven.
>
> Blessed are those who mourn: for they will be comforted.
>
> Blessed are the meek: for they will inherit the earth . . . (Matthew 5:3–5)

"Blessed are the X: for Y" is the formula. It is not rephrased in each case, like "Also, those who are X will be consecrated, because Y." Instead, each sentence has exactly the same structure and exactly the same phrasing.

Do the same for your arguments.

NO:

> When you learn to care for a pet, you learn to attend to the needs of a dependent creature. Watching and responding carefully when a cat or a dog needs you, your ability to recognize needs and adjust your behavior accordingly can improve toward young children as well. Becoming a more responsive keeper of domestic animals can therefore enhance your familial caregiving skills too.

Huh? Each sentence may be fairly clear by itself, but the connections between them are totally lost in the underbrush—interesting underbrush, maybe, but too thick for moving effectively. (Remember, arguments need to *move*!)

YES:

> When you learn to care for a pet, you learn to attend to the needs of a dependent creature. When you learn to attend to the needs of a dependent creature, you learn to be a better parent. Therefore, when you learn to care for a pet, you learn to be a better parent.

The "Yes" version might not be stylish in a flowery way, but it more than makes up for that by being absolutely crystal clear. One simple feature makes the difference: the "No" version uses a new phrase for each key idea every time the idea recurs—for example, "When you learn to care for a pet" is described again in the "No" version's conclusion as "Becoming a more responsive keeper of domestic animals"—whereas the "Yes" argument carefully and exactly repeats its key terms.

If you are concerned about style—as sometimes you should be, of course—then go for the tightest argument, not the most flowery.

MOST CONCISE:

> When you learn to care for a pet, you learn to attend to the needs of a dependent creature, and therefore in turn learn to be a better parent.

II

Arguments by Example

Some arguments offer one or more examples in support of a generalization.

> Women in earlier times were married very young. Juliet in Shakespeare's *Romeo and Juliet* was not even fourteen years old. In the Middle Ages, thirteen was the normal age of marriage for a Jewish woman. And during the Roman Empire, many Roman women were married at age thirteen or younger.

This argument generalizes from three examples—Juliet, Jewish women in the Middle Ages, and Roman women during the Roman Empire—to "many" or *most* women in earlier times. To show the form of this argument most clearly, we can list the premises separately, with the conclusion on the "bottom line":

> Juliet in Shakespeare's play was not even fourteen years old.

> Jewish women during the Middle Ages were normally married at thirteen.

> Many Roman women during the Roman Empire were married at age thirteen or younger.

> Therefore, women in earlier times were married very young.

It is helpful to write short arguments in this way when we need to see exactly how they work.

When do premises like these adequately support a generalization? One requirement, of course, is that the examples be accurate. Remember Rule 3: start from reliable premises! If Juliet *wasn't* around fourteen, or if most Roman or Jewish women *weren't* married at thirteen or younger, then the argument is much weaker. If none of the premises can be supported, there is no argument at all. To check an argument's examples, or to find good examples for your own arguments, you may need to do some research.

But suppose the examples *are* accurate. Even then, generalizing from them is a tricky business. The rules in this chapter offer a short checklist for assessing arguments by example.

7 Use more than one example

A single example can sometimes be used for the sake of *illustration*. The example of Juliet alone might illustrate early marriage. But a single example offers next to no *support* for a generalization. Juliet alone may just be an exception. One spectacularly miserable billionaire does not prove that rich people in general are unhappy. One great meal at a new restaurant in town does not necessarily mean that its whole menu is first-rate. More than one example is needed.

NO:

> Solar power is widely used.
>
> Therefore, renewable energy is widely used.

Solar power is *one* form of renewable energy, but only one. What about others?

YES:

> Solar power is widely used.
>
> Hydroelectric power has long been widely used.
>
> Windmills were once widely used and are becoming widely used again.
>
> Therefore, renewable energy is widely used.

The "Yes" version may not be perfect (Rule 11 returns to it), but it certainly is more energetic, so to speak, than the "No" version.

In a generalization about a small set of things, the strongest argument should consider all, or at least many, of the examples. A generalization about your siblings should consider each of them in turn, for instance, and a generalization about all the planets in the solar system can do the same.

Generalizations about larger sets of things require picking out a *sample*. We cannot list all women in earlier times who married young. Instead, our argument must offer a few women in earlier times as a sample of all women in earlier times. How many examples are required depends partly on how representative they are, a point the next rule takes up. It also depends partly on the size of the set being generalized about. Large sets usually require more examples. The claim that your town is full of remarkable people requires more evidence than the claim that, say, your friends are remarkable people. Depending on how many friends you have, even just two or three examples might be enough to establish that your friends are remarkable people; but, unless your town is tiny, many more examples are required to show that your town is full of remarkable people.

8 Use representative examples

Even a large number of examples may misrepresent the set of things being generalized about. Do all insects bite, for example? Sure, we can think of lots of insects that do, like mosquitoes and black flies, and naturally those are the examples we think of first. After all, we are bugged by them! We may have to consult a biology textbook or a good online source to remember how many kinds of insects there are that *don't* bite—which is most of them, actually: moths, praying mantis, ladybugs, (most) beetles, and so on.

Likewise, a large number of examples of ancient Roman women establishes very little about women generally, since ancient Roman women are not necessarily representative of other women in earlier times. If we want to make a sweeping claim about women in earlier times, the argument needs to consider women from other early times and from other parts of the world as well.

It is easy to overlook how *un*representative—often wildly unrepresentative—our personal "samples" often are. Actually, very few if any of us really know a representative sample of other people. Yet we constantly generalize about other people as a group, such as when we make claims about "human nature," or even how our town might vote in the next election.

NO:

> Everyone in my neighborhood favors the School Bond. Therefore, the School Bond is sure to pass.

This argument is weak because single neighborhoods seldom represent the voting population as a whole. A well-to-do neighborhood may favor a cause unpopular with everyone else. Student wards in university towns regularly are carried by candidates who do poorly elsewhere. Besides, we do not always have good evidence even about the views held in a specific neighborhood. The set of people eager to display their political preferences to the world in yard signs, for example, is unlikely to be a representative cross-section of the neighborhood as a whole.

A *good* argument that "The School Bond is sure to win" requires a representative sample of the entire voting population. It is not easy to construct such a sample. In fact, it usually takes professional help, and even professional pollsters regularly predict elections incorrectly. Telephone pollsters used to call landlines, for example, because cell phone numbers are not as publicly accessible; but only certain demographic groups still have landlines, and they are increasingly unrepresentative.

In general, look for the most accurate cross-section you can find of the population being generalized about. If you want to know what students think about some subject at your university, don't just ask your friends or generalize from what you hear in class. Unless you have quite a range of friends and take a wide range of classes, your personal sample is very unlikely to accurately mirror the whole student body. Similarly, if you want to know what people in other countries think about the United States, don't just ask foreign tourists—for they, of course, are the ones who chose to come here. A careful look at a diverse range of foreign media should give you a more representative picture.

When your sample is people, an even more basic point is that no one should be able to self-select for it. This immediately disqualifies almost all online or mail-in polls to which individuals can decide whether to respond or not. Again, the set of people who are willing or eager to express their opinions is almost certainly not representative of the whole population, but are the people more likely to have strong opinions—or a lot of time on their hands. It may be interesting to know what that group thinks anyway, but not because they necessarily speak for anyone but themselves.

9. Background rates are often crucial

To persuade you that I am a first-rate archer, it is not enough to show you a bull's-eye I have made. You should ask (politely, to be sure), "Yes, but how many times did you *miss*?" Getting a bull's-eye in one shot tells quite a different story than getting a bull's-eye in, say, a thousand, even though in both cases I genuinely do have a bull's-eye to my name. You need a little more data.

> Leon's horoscope told him that he would meet a vivacious new stranger, and lo and behold he did! Therefore, horoscopes are reliable.

Dramatic as such an example may be, the problem is that we are only looking at one case in which a horoscope came true. To properly evaluate this evidence, we need to know something else as well: how many horoscopes *didn't* come true. When I survey my classes, we can usually find a few Leons out of twenty or thirty students. It's a fun moment. But the other nineteen or twenty-nine horoscopes go nowhere. A kind of prediction that comes true only once out of twenty or thirty tries is hardly reliable—it's just lucky once in a while. It may have some dramatic successes, like my archery, but its success *rate* may still be abysmal.

To evaluate the reliability of any argument featuring a few vivid examples, then, we need to know the ratio between the number of "hits," so to speak, and the number of tries. It's a question of representativeness again. Are the featured examples the only ones there are? Is the rate impressively high or low?

This rule is widely applicable. Today, many people live in fear of crime, or constantly attend to stories of shark attacks, terrorism, or other dramatic events. Of course these things are awful when they occur, but the probability of any of them actually happening to any given individual—say, the shark attack *rate*—is extremely low. Crime rates continue to go down.

No doubt we are preoccupied with the exceptions because they are constantly featured on TV and in the news. This does not mean that they are actually representative. The same goes, by the way, for desired things, like winning the lottery. Any individual's chance of winning—that is, the winning *rate*—is so low as to be basically nil, but we seldom see the hundreds of thousands of losers, just the one or few winners raking in the money. So we wildly overestimate the background rates, and imagine that with the next lottery ticket purchase, we may be the one. Save your money, friends. Background rates make all the difference!

10 Statistics need a critical eye

You *cannot* "prove anything with numbers"! Some people see numbers—any numbers—in an argument and conclude from that fact alone that it must be a good argument. Statistics seem to have an aura of authority and definiteness (and did you know that 88 percent of doctors agree?). In fact, though, numbers take as much critical thinking as any other kind of evidence. Don't turn off your brain!

> After an era when some athletic powerhouse universities were accused of exploiting student athletes, leaving them to flunk out once their eligibility expired, college athletes are now graduating at higher rates. Many schools are now graduating more than 50 percent of their athletes.

Fifty percent, eh? Pretty impressive! But this figure, at first so persuasive, does not really do the job it claims to do.

First, although "many" schools graduate more than 50 percent of their athletes, it appears that some do not—so this figure may well exclude the most exploitative schools that really concerned people in the first place.

The argument does offer graduation rates. But it would be useful to know how a "more than 50 percent" graduation rate compares with the graduation rate for *all* students at the same institutions. If it is significantly lower, athletes may still be getting the shaft.

Most importantly, this argument offers no reason to believe that college athletes' graduation rates are actually *improving*, because no comparison to any previous rate is offered! The conclusion claims that the graduation rate is now "higher," but without knowing the previous rates it is impossible to tell.

Numbers may offer incomplete evidence in other ways too. Rule 9, for example, tells us that knowing background rates may be crucial. Correspondingly, when an argument offers rates or percentages, the relevant background information usually must include the *number* of examples. Car thefts on campus may have doubled, but if this means that two cars were stolen rather than one, there's not much to worry about.

Another statistical pitfall is *over-precision*:

> Every year this campus wastes 412,067 paper and plastic cups. It's time to switch to reusable cups!

I'm all for ending waste too, and I'm sure the amount of campus waste is huge. But no one really knows the precise number of cups wasted—and it's extremely unlikely to be exactly the same every year. Here the appearance of exactness makes the evidence seem more authoritative than it really is.

Be wary, also, of numbers that are easily manipulated. Pollsters know very well that the way a question is asked can shape how it is answered. These days we are even seeing "polls" that try to change people's minds about, say, a political candidate, just by asking loaded questions ("If you were to discover that she is a liar and a cheat, how would that change your vote?"). Then too, many apparently "hard" statistics are actually based on guesswork or extrapolation, such as data about semi-legal or illegal activities. Since people have a major motive not to reveal or report things like drug use, under-the-counter transactions, hiring illegal aliens, and the like, beware of any confident generalizations about how widespread they are.

Yet again:

> If kids keep watching more TV at current rates, by 2025 they'll have no time left to sleep!

Right, and by 2040 they'll be watching thirty-six hours a day. Extrapolation in such cases is perfectly possible mathematically, but after a certain point it tells you nothing.

11 Reckon with counterexamples

Counterexamples are examples that contradict your generalization. No fun—maybe. But counterexamples actually can be a generalizer's best friends, if you use them early and use them well. Exceptions don't "prove the rule"—quite the contrary, they threaten to *dis*prove it—but they can and should prompt us to *refine* it. Therefore, seek out counterexamples early and systematically. It is the best way to sharpen your own generalizations and to probe more deeply into your theme.

Consider this argument once again:

> Solar power is widely used.
>
> Hydroelectric power has long been widely used.
>
> Windmills were once widely used and are becoming widely used again.
>
> Therefore, renewable energy is widely used.

The examples here certainly do help to show that *many* renewable energy sources are widely used: sun, wind, and rain. However, as soon as you start thinking about counterexamples instead of just more examples, you may find that the argument somewhat overgeneralizes.

Are *all* renewables widely used? Look up the definition of "re-newable energy" and you will find that there are other types as well, such as the tides and geothermal energy (the internal heat of the earth). And these, for better or worse, are not so widely used. They aren't available everywhere, for one thing, and may be difficult to harness even when available.

When you think of counterexamples to a generalization that you want to defend, then you need to adjust your generalization. If the re-newable energy argument were yours, for instance, you might change the conclusion to *"Many forms of* renewable energy are widely used." Your argument still hits the high points, so to speak, while it acknow-ledges limits and the possibility for improvement in some areas.

Counterexamples should prompt you to think more deeply about what you actually want to say. For example, maybe your interest in arguing about renewables is to try to show that there are ready and workable alternatives to the usual non-renewable sources. If that is your aim, you don't necessarily need to argue that *all* renewables are widely used. It is enough that *some* are. You might even urge that the ones that are less widely used be better developed.

Or, instead of arguing that every renewable source is or could be widely used, you might really want to be arguing that every (or most every?) place has at least some renewable source available to it, though there may be different sources in different places. This is a quite different and more subtle claim than the original, and gives your thinking some interesting room to move. (Might this argument have counterexamples too? I leave that question for you.)

Ask yourself about counterexamples when you are assessing others' arguments as well as evaluating your own. Ask whether *their* conclusions might have to be revised and limited, or rethought in more subtle and complex directions. The same rules apply both to others' arguments and to yours. The only difference is that you have a chance to correct your overgeneralizations yourself.

III

Arguments by Analogy

There is an exception to Rule 7 ("Use more than one example"). Arguments by analogy, rather than multiplying examples to support a generalization, argue from *one* specific example to another, reasoning that because the two examples are alike in many ways, they are also alike in one further specific way.

Valentina Tereshkova, Russian astronaut and first woman in space, famously quipped that

> If women can be railroad workers in Russia, why can't they fly in space?

Russian women are as capable of demanding physical and technical work as men, Tereshkova is arguing, and as devoted to their work and their country—as proved by the example of female railroad workers. Therefore, women should also make fine astronauts. Spelled out, the argument looks like this:

> Women have proved themselves to be capable railroad workers in Russia.
>
> Being a railroad worker is *like* being an astronaut (because they both make extreme physical and technical demands).
>
> Therefore, women can be capable astronauts as well.

Notice the italicized word "like" in the second premise. When an argument stresses the likeness between two cases, it is very probably an argument from analogy.

12

Analogies require relevantly similar examples

How do we evaluate arguments by analogy?

The first premise of an argument by analogy makes a claim about the example used as an analogy. Remember Rule 3: make sure this premise is true. Tereshkova's argument could not even get off the ground, so to speak, if women had *not* proved themselves to be capable railroad workers in Russia.

The second premise in arguments by analogy claims that the example in the first premise is *like* the example about which the argument draws a conclusion. Evaluating this premise requires us to ask how relevantly similar the two cases are.

They do not have to be similar in *every* way. After all, being an astronaut is very different than working on the railroad. Trains don't fly, for example—or when they do, the story does not have a happy ending. Astronauts better not wield sledgehammers. But argument by analogy only requires *relevant* similarities. Technical skill and physical strength and stamina seem to be Tereshkova's real themes. Both astronauts and railroad workers require a lot of both.

So how relevantly similar, in the end, is Tereshkova's analogy? For modern astronauts, you might think that sheer physical stamina is less relevant than skill at running experiments and making scientific observations—skills not necessarily related to being a good railroad worker. In Tereshkova's time, however, physical strength and stamina were much more important, as was body size: the early capsules were quite small and actually suited women's physiques better. The other key factor was that the early Russian astronauts had to eject from their capsule and parachute to the ground at the end of their missions—and Tereshkova was a champion parachutist. This was probably the key factor, and is related to strength and stamina, though not to railroad work.

Tereshkova's analogy partially succeeds, then, especially for her time, though it is less persuasive now. But of course, since there have now been many successful female astronauts, it is also less necessary.

Here is a more challenging argument from analogy.

> An interesting switch was pulled in Rome yesterday by Adam Nordwell, an American Chippewa chief. As he descended his plane from California dressed in full tribal regalia, Nordwell announced in the name of the American Indian people that he was taking possession of Italy "by right of discovery" in the same way that Christopher Columbus did in America. "I proclaim this day the day of the discovery of Italy," said Nordwell. "What right did Columbus have to discover America when it had already been inhabited for thousands of years? The same right I now have to come to Italy and proclaim the discovery of your country."[2]

Nordwell is suggesting that his "discovery" of Italy is *like* Columbus's "discovery" of America in at least one important way: both Nordwell and Columbus claimed a country that already had been inhabited by its own people for centuries. Thus, Nordwell insists that he has as much "right" to claim Italy as Columbus had to claim America. But, of course, Nordwell has no right at all to claim Italy. It follows that Columbus had no right at all to claim America.

> Nordwell has no right to claim Italy for another people, let alone "by right of discovery" (because Italy has been inhabited by its own people for centuries).

> Columbus's claim to America "by right of discovery" is *like* Nordwell's claim to Italy (America, too, had been inhabited by its own people for centuries).

> Therefore, Columbus had no right to claim America for another people, let alone "by right of discovery."

How good is Nordwell's analogy? Obviously, twentieth-century Italy is not just like fifteenth-century America. Italy is known to every twentieth-century schoolchild, whereas America was unknown to much of the world in the fifteenth century. Nordwell is not an explorer, and a commercial jet is not the *Santa Maria*. But are these differences relevant to Nordwell's analogy? Nordwell simply means to remind us that it is senseless to claim a country already inhabited

---

2. *Miami News*, 23 September 1973.

by its own people. Whether that land is known to the world's school-children, or how the "discoverer" arrived there, is not important. The more appropriate reaction might have been to try to establish diplomatic relations, as we would try to do today if somehow the land and people of Italy had just been discovered. *That's* Nordwell's point, and, taken in that way, his analogy makes a good (and unsettling) argument.

IV

Arguments from Authority

No one can be an expert through direct experience on everything there is to know. We do not live in ancient times ourselves and therefore cannot know first-hand at what age women tended to marry back then. Few of us have enough experience to judge which kinds of cars are safest in a crash. We do not know first-hand what is really happening in Sri Lanka or the state legislature, or even in the average American classroom or street corner. Instead, we must rely on others—better-situated people, organizations, surveys, or reference works—to tell us much of what we need to know about the world. We argue like this:

> X (a source that ought to know) says that Y.
>
> Therefore, Y is true.

For instance:

> Dr. Aubrey de Grey says that people can live to be 1,000 years old.
>
> Therefore, people can live to be 1,000 years old.

It's a risky business, though. Supposed experts may be overconfident (they're human too), or may be misled, or may not even be reliable. And everyone has biases, after all, even if innocent ones. Once again we must consider a checklist of standards that truly authoritative sources need to meet.

13

Cite your sources

Who's got your back?

Some factual assertions are so obvious or well known that they do not need support at all. It is usually not necessary to prove that the United States currently has fifty states or that Juliet loved Romeo. However, a precise figure for the current population of the United States, say, does need a citation. Likewise, to develop Valentina Tereshkova's argument for sending women to space, we'd need to find knowledgeable authorities to establish that women were indeed capable railroad workers in Russia.

NO:

> I once read that there are cultures in which makeup and clothes are mostly men's business, not women's.

If you're arguing about whether men and women everywhere follow the gender roles familiar to us, this is a relevant example—a striking case of different gender roles. But few of us know anything about this sort of difference first-hand, and it will probably seem surprising and even unlikely to many people. To nail down the argument, then, you need to call upon a fully cited source.

YES:

> Carol Beckwith's classic study of "Niger's Wodaabe" (*National Geographic* 164, no. 4 [October 1983], pp. 483–509) reports that among the West African Fulani peoples such as the Wodaabe, makeup and clothes are mostly men's business.

Citation styles vary—consult a handbook of style to find the appropriate format for your purposes—but all include the same basic information: enough so that others can easily find the source on their own.

14

Seek informed sources

Who knows?

Sources must be qualified to make the statements they make. Honda mechanics are qualified to discuss the merits of different Hondas, midwives and obstetricians are qualified to discuss pregnancy and childbirth, teachers are qualified to discuss the state of their schools, and so on. These sources are qualified because they have the appropriate background and information. For the best information about global climate change, go to climatologists, not politicians.

Where a source's qualifications are not immediately clear, an argument must explain them. Dr. Aubrey de Grey says that people can live to be 1,000 years old? Well, who is this Aubrey de Grey to expect us to believe him about such things? Here is an answer: He is a gerontologist who has developed detailed theories of the causes of aging (it is *not* inevitable, he argues) and possible preventive interventions, which he has laid out in several detailed books such as *The Mitochondrial Free Radical Theory of Aging* (Cambridge University Press, 1999), for which he was awarded a PhD in biology by Cambridge University in 2000. When someone like *that* says that people can live to be 1,000 years old—unlikely as it seems—it is not a random or unprofessional opinion. We should give him a serious hearing.

As you explain your source's qualifications, you can also add more direct evidence to your argument.

> Carol Beckwith's classic study of "Niger's Wodaabe" (*National Geographic* 164, no. 4 [October 1983], pp. 483–509) reports that among the West African Fulani peoples such as the Wodaabe, makeup and clothes are mostly men's business. Beckwith and an anthropologist colleague lived with the Wodaabe for two years and observed many dances for which the men prepared by lengthy preening, face-painting, and teeth-whitening. (Her article includes many pictures too.) Wodaabe women watch, comment, and choose mates for their beauty—which the men say is the natural way. "Our beauty makes the women want us," one says.

Note that an informed source need not fit our general stereotype of an "authority"—and a person who fits our stereotype of an authority may not even be an informed source. If you're checking out colleges, for instance, students are the best authorities, not administrators or recruiters, because it's the students who know what student life is really like. (Just be sure to find yourself a representative sample.)

Note also that experts on one subject are not necessarily informed about every subject on which they offer opinions.

> Beyoncé is a vegan. Therefore, veganism is the best diet.

Beyoncé may be a fabulous entertainer, but a diet expert she's not. (Also, it is not entirely clear that she *is* a vegan, apparently.) Likewise, just because someone can put the title "Doctor" before their name—that is, just because they have a PhD or MD in some field—does not mean that they are qualified to deliver opinions on any subject whatsoever.

Sometimes we must rely on sources whose knowledge is better than ours but still limited in various ways. On occasion, the best information we can get about what is happening in a war zone or a political trial or inside a business or bureaucracy is fragmentary and filtered through journalists, international human rights organizations, corporate watchdogs, and so on. If you must rely on a source that may have limited knowledge in this way, acknowledge the problem. Let your readers or hearers decide whether imperfect authority is better than none at all.

Truly informed sources rarely expect others to accept their conclusions simply because they assert them. Good sources will offer at least some reasons or evidence—examples, facts, analogies, other kinds of arguments—to help explain and defend their conclusions. Beckwith, for example, offers photographs and stories from the years she lived with the Wodaabe. Thus, while we might need to take some of their *specific* claims on authority alone (for instance, we must take Beckwith at her word that she had certain experiences), we can expect even the best sources to offer arguments as well as their own judgments in support of their general conclusions. Look for those arguments, then, and look at them critically as well.

15

Seek impartial sources

People who have the most at stake in a dispute are usually not the best sources of information about the issues involved. Sometimes they may not even tell the truth. People accused in criminal trials are presumed innocent until proven guilty, but we seldom completely believe their claims of innocence without confirmation from impartial witnesses.

Readiness to tell the truth as one sees it, though, is not always enough. The truth as one honestly sees it can still be biased. We tend to see what we expect to see. We notice, remember, and pass on information that supports our point of view, but we may not be quite so motivated when the evidence points the other way.

Therefore, look for *impartial* sources: people or organizations who do not have a stake in the immediate issue, and who have a prior and primary interest in accuracy, such as (some) university scientists or statistical databases. Don't just rely on politicians or interest groups on *one* side of a major public question for the most accurate information about the issues at stake. Don't just rely on manufacturers' advertisements for reliable information concerning their products.

NO:

> My car dealer recommends that I pay $300 to rustproof my car. He should know; I guess I'd better do it.

He probably *does* know, but he might not be entirely reliable, either. The best information about consumer products and services comes from independent consumer testing agencies, agencies not affiliated with any manufacturer or provider but answering to consumers who want the most accurate information they can get. Do some research!

YES:

> Experts at *Consumer Reports* say that rust problems have almost vanished in modern cars due to better manufacturing,

and advise that rustproofing is not needed (*Consumer Reports*, "Watch Out for These Car Sales Tricks," http://www
.consumerreports.org/buying-a-car/car-sales-tricks/, 2 February 2017; and Sami Haaj-Assaad, "Should You Rust Proof
Your New Car?" Auto-Guide.com, 21 March 2013).

On political matters, especially when the disagreements are basically over statistics, look to independent government agencies, such as the Census Bureau, or to university studies or other independent sources. Organizations like Doctors Without Borders are relatively impartial sources on the human rights situation in other countries because they practice medicine, not politics: they are not trying to support or oppose any specific government.

Of course, independence and impartiality are not always easy to judge, either. Be sure that your sources are *genuinely* independent and not just interest groups masquerading under an independent-sounding name. Check who funds them; check their other publications; look for their track record; watch the tone of their statements. Sources that make extreme or simplistic claims, or spend most of their time attacking and demeaning the other side, weaken their own claims. Again, seek out sources that offer constructive arguments and responsibly acknowledge and thoroughly engage the arguments and evidence on the other side. At the very least, try to confirm for yourself any factual claim quoted from a potentially biased source. Good arguments cite their sources (Rule 13); look them up. Make sure the evidence is quoted correctly and not pulled out of context, and check for further information that might be helpful.

16 Cross-check sources
Don't bet on a one-off

Consult and compare a variety of sources to see if other, equally good authorities agree. Are the experts sharply divided or in agreement? If they're pretty much in agreement, theirs is the safe view to take—and the opposite view is, at the very least, unwise, however strongly it may appeal to us. Authoritative views can certainly be wrong at times. But *non*authoritative views are *regularly* wrong.

On the other hand, cross-checking may sometimes reveal that the experts themselves disagree on some subject. In that case, reserve judgment yourself. Don't jump in with two feet where truly informed people tread with care. Better to argue on some other grounds—or rethink your conclusions.

What about our friend Aubrey de Grey, then, and our hopes of living 1,000 years? Alas, when you start to cross-check, it turns out that de Grey's work is widely regarded as well-developed and his research as certainly worth pursuing, but very few other experts are persuaded.[3] Many are sharply critical. He's an outlier. Living vastly longer may be an appealing thought, but don't count it very likely.

On most significant topics you can probably find *some* disagreement if you look hard enough. Worse, on some topics the appearance of controversy may be created even when there is virtually no disagreement among qualified authorities. Although there was a time when experts disagreed about global climate change, for example, the world scientific community is now nearly unanimous that the climate is changing and that human activity has something to do with it. Sure, there's still loud disagreement in some media and election campaigns, but virtually none among trained climate scientists looking at the data as objectively as they can. There are also a few reasoned critiques of the climate-change consensus, but in the best judgment of almost everyone actually in the field, they do not change the bottom line. Some of the critiques have even sharpened the science, but the critics, even when qualified, are (very markedly) outliers.

Ideology seems to be the driving force here—not actual evidence or professional judgment. You may need to look into seeming controversies like these to see how seriously to take them.[4]

---

3. For de Grey's popular presentation of his theories, see his book *Ending Aging: The Rejuvenation Breakthroughs That Could Reverse Human Aging in our Lifetimes* (St. Martins Griffin, 2008). A highly critical response by a group of fellow gerontologists is Huber Warner, et al., "Science Fact and the SENS Agenda," *EMBO Reports* 2005 (6): 1006–1008, http://embor.embopress.org/content/6/11/1006.

4. For a contemporary summary of the state of climate science, also addressing some skeptical claims, start with G. Thomas Farmer's short textbook *Modern Climate Change Science* (Springer, 2015). Of course, once again, the consensus of experts *may* be wrong. Still, expert agreement is usually the best we can do. Even climate change "deniers" would not, say, go against the unanimous advice of their doctors if they were to learn that they might be seriously ill. They would not, so to say, bet their life that all their

17

Build your Internet savvy

Online, even the most baseless or hateful opinion site can dress itself up to look plausible and even professional. Academic book publishers and even most public libraries have at least some checks on the reliability and tone of the books and other materials they collect, but on the Internet, it is still the Wild West—no checks. You're on your own.

"The Internet" by itself, in any case, is not any kind of authority. It merely transmits other sources. Savvy users know how to evaluate those sources—they apply the rules in this book. Rule 13, for example: What *is* the source? With many websites this may be difficult to tell—and that's a red flag right there. Are the sources well-informed (Rule 14)? Reliable (15)? Or are the sites pushing an agenda—trying to sell you something, or to manipulate your view on some issues by, say, using loaded language (5), unrepresentative data (8), or outlying or phony "experts" (14 and 16)? At minimum, cross-check other, independent websites on the same issue (16).

Savvy users also dig deeper than the standard Web search. Search engines cannot search "everything"—far from it. In fact, the most reliable and detailed information on any given topic is often found in databases or other academic resources that standard search engines cannot enter at all. You may need a password; ask your teacher or librarian.

Savvy users may also—cautiously!—consult Wikipedia. It's certainly true that "anyone can edit Wikipedia," as is often objected, and as a result false and defamatory information has sometimes been posted. Subtle biases surely persist. Still, Wikipedia's very openness

---

doctors are wrong, no matter how fervently they might wish it. But they would have us bet the future of Earth itself that the consensus of climate experts is wrong? Current efforts on the part of some politicians to shut down climate research, and even to prevent scientists from communicating with the public or public agencies from planning for climate-change adaptation, are even worse: they reveal not a constructive and evidence-based skepticism, but (it seems) just the opposite. Even responsible denial needs evidence!

can also be an advantage. Every article is subject to constant scrutiny and correction by other users. Many users are moved to contribute additional information or improvements too. Over time, many articles tend to become more comprehensive and neutral. Wikipedian editors sometimes intervene if there is too much contention, and some hot-topic articles are not open to general editing, but the end result is that Wikipedia's error *rate* (remember Rule 9!) has been compared favorably even to the *Encyclopedia Britannica*.[5]

Of course, savvy encyclopedia users know that they cannot simply cite Wikipedia (or, usually, any other encyclopedia) to back up their claims. Wikipedia's intention is to organize and summarize knowledge on a subject, and then to point readers to the real sources. Savvy users also remain watchful—as in *any* source—for subtle hints of loaded language, dismissive accounts of disfavored views, and the like.

Every reference source is a product of a group of people with their limits and biases, acknowledged and unacknowledged. At least as important as avoiding mistakes or bias is having a means of correcting them—and fast—and at that Wikipedia is unexcelled. Random insertions and vandalism are typically repaired within minutes, and every change is tracked and explained (check out every page's "View History" tab) and sometimes widely debated as well (check out the "Talk" tabs). What other reference source is so transparent and self-correcting? *Really* savvy users might join the work of making Wikipedia still better!

---

5. See Jim Giles, "Internet Encyclopedias Go Head to Head," *Nature* 438 (7070): 900–1, December 2005. The March 2006 issue of *Nature* includes a response from *Encyclopedia Britannica* and a rejoinder from *Nature*.

V

Arguments about Causes

Did you know that students who sit at the front of the classroom tend to get better grades? And that people who are married are, on average, happier than people who aren't? Wealth, by contrast, doesn't seem to correlate with happiness at all—so maybe it is true after all that "the best things in life are free." If you'd rather have the money anyway, you might be interested to know that people with "can-do" attitudes tend to be wealthier. So you'd better work on your attitude, eh?

Here we come to arguments about causes and their effects—about what causes what. Such arguments are often vital. Good effects we want to increase, bad effects we want to prevent, and we often want to give appropriate credit or blame for both. It won't surprise you, though, that reasoning about causes also takes care and critical thinking.

 ## Causal arguments start with correlations

The evidence for a claim about causes is usually a *correlation*—a regular association—between two events or kinds of events: between your grades in a class and where you sit in the classroom; between being married and being happy; between the unemployment rate and the crime rate, etc. The general form of the argument therefore is:

> Event or condition E_1 is *regularly associated* with event or condition E_2.

> Therefore, event or condition E_1 *causes* event or condition E_2.

That is, *because* E_1 is regularly associated with E_2 in this way, we conclude that E_1 causes E_2. For example:

People who meditate tend to be calmer.

Therefore, meditation calms you down.

Trends may also be correlated, as when we note that increasing violence on television correlates with increasing violence in the real world.

Shows on television portray more and more violence, callousness, and depravity—and society is becoming more and more violent, callous, and depraved.

Therefore, television is ruining our morals.

Inverse correlations (that is, where an increase in one factor correlates to a *decrease* in another) may suggest causality too. For example, some studies correlate increased vitamin use with decreased health, suggesting that vitamins may (sometimes) be harmful. In the same way, *non*correlation may imply *lack* of cause, as when we discover that happiness and wealth are not correlated and therefore conclude that money does not bring happiness.

Exploring correlations is also a scientific research strategy. What causes lightning? Why do some people become insomniacs, or geniuses, or Republicans? And isn't there *some* way (please?) to prevent colds? Researchers look for correlates to these conditions of interest: that is, for other conditions or events that are regularly associated with lightning or genius or colds, for example, but without which lightning or genius or colds don't tend to happen. These correlates may be subtle and complex, but finding them is often possible nonetheless— and then (hopefully) we have a handle on causes.

19 Correlations may have alternative explanations

Arguments from correlation to cause are often compelling. However, there is also a systematic difficulty with any such claim. The problem is simply that *any correlation may be explained in multiple ways.* It's often not clear from the correlation itself how best to interpret the underlying causes.

First, some correlations may simply be coincidental. For example, though the Seattle Seahawks and the Denver Broncos both went to the Super Bowl in the same year that their home states legalized marijuana—2012—it's not likely that these events were actually connected.

Second, even when there really is a connection, correlation by itself does not establish the *direction* of the connection. If E_1 is correlated with E_2, E_1 may cause E_2—but E_2 may instead cause E_1. For example, while it is true (on average) that people with "can-do" attitudes tend to be wealthier, it's not at all clear that the attitude leads to the wealth. It may be more plausible the other way around: that the wealth causes the attitude. You're more apt to believe in the possibility of success when you've already been successful. Wealth and attitude may correlate, then, but if you want to get wealthier, just working on your attitude may not get you very far.

Likewise, it's entirely possible that calmer people tend to be drawn to meditation, rather than becoming calmer *because* they meditate. And the very same correlation that suggests that television is "ruining our morals" could instead suggest that our morals are ruining television (that is, that rising real-world violence is leading to an increase in the portrayal of violence on television).

Third, some other cause may underlie and explain both of the correlates. Again E_1 may be correlated with E_2, but rather than E_1 causing E_2 *or* E_2 causing E_1, something else—some E_3—may cause both E_1 and E_2. For example, the fact that students who sit in the front of the classroom tend to get better grades may not imply *either* that sitting in the front leads to better grades *or* that getting better grades leads to sitting in the front of the class. More likely, some students' special commitment to making the most of their schooling leads *both* to sitting in the front of the classroom *and* to better grades.

Finally, multiple or complex causes may be at work, and they may move in many directions at the same time. Violence on television, for example, surely reflects a more violent state of society, but also, to some degree, it surely helps to worsen that violence. Quite likely there are other underlying causes as well, such as the breakup of traditional value systems and the absence of constructive pastimes.

Work toward the most likely explanation

Since a variety of explanations for a correlation are usually possible, the challenge for a good correlation-based argument is to find the most *likely* explanation.

First, fill in the connections. That is, spell out how each possible explanation could make sense.

NO:

> Independent filmmakers generally make more creative films than the big studios. Thus, their independence leads to their creativity.

There's a correlation, yes, but the causal conclusion is a little abrupt. What's the connection?

YES:

> Independent filmmakers generally make more creative films than the big studios. It makes sense that with less studio control, independent filmmakers are freer to try new things for more varied audiences. Independents also usually have much less money at stake, and therefore can afford for a creative experiment to fall flat. Thus, their independence leads to their creativity.

Next, try to fill in the connections in this way not just for the explanation you favor, but also for alternative explanations. For example, consider studies that correlate increased vitamin use with decreased health. One possible explanation is that vitamins actually worsen health, or anyway that some vitamins (or taking a lot of them) are bad for some people. It is also possible, though, that people who already are in bad or worsening health may be using more vitamins to try to get better. In fact, this alternative explanation seems, at least at first glance, equally or even more plausible.

Finally, try to decide which is the most likely explanation for the correlation. You may need more information. In particular, is there other evidence that (some?) vitamins can sometimes be harmful? If so, how widespread might these harms be? If there is little direct and specific evidence of harm to be found, especially when vitamins are taken in appropriate dosages, then it's more likely that poorer health leads to more vitamin use than that more vitamin use leads to poorer health.

Or again: Marriage and happiness correlate (again, on average), but is it because marriage makes you happier or because happier people tend to be more successful at getting and staying married? Fill in the connections for both explanations and then step back to think.

Marriage clearly offers companionship and support, which could explain how marriage might make you happier. Conversely, it may be that happy people are better at getting and staying married. To me, though, this second explanation seems less likely. Happiness may make you a more appealing partner, but then again it may not—it could instead make you more self-absorbed—and it is not clear that happiness by itself makes you any more committed or responsive a partner. I'd prefer the first explanation.

Note that the most likely explanation is very seldom some sort of conspiracy or supernatural intervention. It is *possible*, of course, that the Bermuda Triangle really is spooked and that is why ships and planes disappear there. But that explanation is far less likely than another simple and natural explanation: that the Bermuda Triangle is one of the world's heaviest-traveled shipping and sailing areas, with tropical weather that is unpredictable and sometimes severe. Besides, people do tend to embellish spooky stories, so some of the more lurid accounts, having passed through countless retellings, aren't (let's just say) the most reliable.

Likewise, although people fasten onto inconsistencies and oddities in dramatic events (the JFK assassination, 9/11, etc.) to justify conspiracy theories, such explanations usually leave a great deal more *un*explained than the usual explanations, however incomplete. (For instance, why would any plausible conspiracy take *this particular form*?) Don't assume that every little oddity must have some nefarious explanation. It's hard enough to get the basics right. Neither you nor anyone else needs to have an answer for everything.

21

Expect complexity

Plenty of happy people are not married, of course, and plenty of married people are unhappy. Still, it does not follow that marriage has no effect on happiness *on average*. It's just that happiness and unhappiness (and, for that matter, being married or unmarried) have many other causes too. One correlation is not the whole story. The question in such cases is about the *relative weight* of different causes.

If you or someone else has argued that some E_1 causes some E_2, it is not necessarily a counterexample if occasionally E_1 doesn't produce E_2, or if another cause entirely may also sometimes produce E_2. The claim is just that E_1 *often* or *usually* produces E_2, and that other causes less commonly do, or that E_1 is among the *major contributors* to E_2, though the full story may involve multiple causes and there may be other major contributors too. There are people who never smoke cigarettes at all and still get lung cancer, and also people who smoke three packs of cigarettes a day and never get it. Both effects are medically intriguing and important, but the fact remains that smoking is the prime cause of lung cancer.

Many different causes may contribute to an overall effect. Though the causes of global climate change are many and varied, for instance, the fact that some of them are natural, such as changes in the sun's brightness, does not show that human contributions therefore have no effect. Once again, the causal story is complex. Many factors are at work. (Indeed, if the sun is *also* contributing to global warming, there's even more reason to try to decrease our contribution.)

Causes and effects may "loop," too. Filmmakers' independence may lead to their creativity, but, then again, creative filmmakers may seek independence from the start, leading to more creativity, and so on. Others may seek both creativity *and* independence because they prefer a less pressured life, or maybe they just have some great idea that they can't sell to a big studio. It's complicated. . . .

VI

Deductive Arguments

Consider this argument:

> If there are no chance factors in chess, then chess is a game of pure skill.
>
> There are no chance factors in chess.
>
> Therefore, chess is a game of pure skill.

Suppose that the premises of this argument are true. In other words, suppose it's true that *if* there are no chance factors in chess, then chess is a game of pure skill—and suppose there *are* no chance factors in chess. You can therefore conclude with perfect assurance that chess is a game of pure skill. There is no way to admit the truth of these premises but deny the conclusion.

Arguments of this type are called *deductive arguments*. That is, a properly formed deductive argument is an argument of such a form that if its premises are true, the conclusion must be true too. Properly formed deductive arguments are called *valid* arguments.

Deductive arguments differ from the sorts of arguments so far considered, in which even a large number of true premises does not guarantee the truth of the conclusion (although sometimes they may make it very likely). In nondeductive arguments, the conclusion unavoidably goes beyond the premises—that's the very point of arguing by example, authority, and so on—whereas the conclusion of a valid deductive argument only makes explicit what is already contained in the premises, though it may not be clear until it is spelled out.

In real life, of course, we can't always be sure of our premises either, so the conclusions of real-life deductive arguments still have to be taken with a few (sometimes many) grains of salt. Still, when strong premises can be found, deductive forms are very useful. And even when the premises are uncertain, deductive forms offer an effective way to organize arguments.

Modus ponens

Using the letters **p** and **q** to stand for declarative sentences, the simplest valid deductive form is

If [sentence **p**] then [sentence **q**].

[Sentence **p**].

Therefore, [sentence **q**].

Or, more briefly:

> If **p** then **q**.
>
> **p**.
>
> Therefore, **q**.

This form is called *modus ponens* ("the mode of putting": put **p**, get **q**). Taking **p** to stand for "There are no chance factors in chess," and **q** to stand for "Chess is a game of pure skill," our introductory example follows *modus ponens* (check it out). Here is another:

> If drivers on cell phones have more accidents, then drivers should be prohibited from using them.
>
> Drivers on cell phones *do* have more accidents.
>
> Therefore, drivers should be prohibited from using cell phones.

To develop this argument, you must explain and defend both of its premises, and they require quite different arguments (go back and look). *Modus ponens* gives you a way to lay them out clearly and separately from the start.

23

Modus tollens

A second valid deductive form is *modus tollens* ("the mode of taking": take **q**, take **p**).

> If **p** then **q**.
>
> Not-**q**.
>
> Therefore, not-**p**.

Here "Not-**q**" simply stands for the denial of **q**, that is, for the sentence "It is not true that **q**." The same is true for "not-**p**."

Want to play detective? Sherlock Holmes used a *modus tollens* argument at a key moment in "The Adventure of Silver Blaze." A horse had been stolen out of a well-guarded barn. The barn had a dog, but the dog did not bark. Now what do we make of that?

> A dog was kept in the stables, and yet, though someone had been in and had fetched out a horse, [the dog] had not barked. . . . Obviously the . . . visitor was someone whom the dog knew well.[6]

Holmes's argument can be put as a *modus tollens*:

> If the visitor were a stranger, then the dog would have barked.
>
> The dog did not bark.
>
> Therefore, the visitor was not a stranger.

To write his deduction in symbols, you could use **s** for "The visitor was a stranger" and **b** for "The dog barked."

> If **s** then **b**.
>
> Not-**b**.
>
> Therefore, not-**s**.

---

6. Sir Arthur Conan Doyle, "The Adventure of Silver Blaze," in *The Complete Sherlock Holmes* (Garden City, NY: Garden City Books, 1930), p. 199.

"Not-**b**" stands for "The dog did not bark," and "not-**s**" stands for "The visitor was not a stranger." As Holmes puts it, the visitor was someone whom the dog knew well. It was an inside job!

Hypothetical syllogism

A third valid deductive form is "hypothetical syllogism."

> If **p** then **q**.
>
> If **q** then **r**.
>
> Therefore, if **p** then **r**.

For instance, remember this argument from Rule 6:

> When you learn to care for a pet, you learn to attend to the needs of a dependent creature. When you learn to attend to the needs of a dependent creature, you learn to be a better parent. Therefore, when you learn to care for a pet, you learn to be a better parent.

Separating out and slightly rephrasing the premises into "if-then" form:

> If you learn to care for a pet, then you learn to attend to the needs of a dependent creature.
>
> If you learn to attend to the needs of a dependent creature, then you learn to be a better parent.
>
> Therefore, if you learn to care for a pet, then you learn to be a better parent.

Using the letters in boldface to stand for the component sentences in these premises, we have:

If **c** then **a**.

If **a** then **p**.

Therefore, if **c** then **p**.

And you see why using consistent terms and phrasing helps so much!

Hypothetical syllogisms are valid for any number of premises, as long as each premise has the form "If **p** then **q**" and the **q** (called the "consequent") of one premise becomes the **p** (the "antecedent") of the next.

Disjunctive syllogism

A fourth valid deductive form is "disjunctive syllogism."

> **p** or **q**.
>
> Not-**p**.
>
> Therefore, **q**.

For example, suppose we continue playing detective:

> Either Dorabella or Fiordiligi stole the tarts. But Dorabella didn't do it. The implication is pretty clear . . .

Using **d** for "Dorabella stole the tarts" and **f** for "Fiordiligi stole the tarts," we have

> Either **d** or **f**.
>
> Not **d**.
>
> Therefore, **f**.

There is one complication. In English the word "or" can have two different meanings. Usually "**p** or **q**" means that at least one of **p** or **q** is true, and possibly both. This is called an "inclusive" sense of the word "or" and is the sense normally assumed in logic. Sometimes, though, we use "or" in an "exclusive" sense, in which "**p** or **q**" means that either **p** or **q** is true but *not* both. "Either they'll come by land or they'll come by sea," for example, suggests that they won't come both ways at once. In that case you might be able to infer that if they come one way, then they're *not* coming the other way (better be sure!).

Disjunctive syllogisms are valid regardless of which sense of "or" is used (check it out). But what *else*, if anything, you may be able to infer from a statement like "**p** or **q**"—in particular, whether you can conclude not-**q** if you also know **p**—depends on the meaning of "or" in the specific "**p** or **q**" premise you are considering. (For example, if we knew only that Dorabella stole the tarts, can we be sure Fiordiligi didn't help?) Take care!

26 Dilemma

A fifth valid deductive form is the "dilemma."

> **p** or **q**.
>
> If **p** then **r**.
>
> If **q** then **s**.
>
> Therefore, **r** or **s**.

Rhetorically, a dilemma is a choice between two options both of which have unappealing consequences. The pessimist philosopher Arthur Schopenhauer, for example, formulated what is sometimes called the "Hedgehog's dilemma," which we could paraphrase like this:

> The closer two hedgehogs get, the more likely they are to poke each other with their spikes; but if they remain apart, they will be lonely. So it is with people: being close to someone inevitably creates conflicts and provocations and opens us to a lot of pain; but on the other hand, we're lonely when we stand apart.

In outline this argument might be put:

> Either we become close to others or we stand apart.
>
> If we become close to others, we suffer conflict and pain.
>
> If we stand apart, we'll be lonely.
>
> Therefore, either we suffer conflict and pain or we'll be lonely.

And in symbols:

> Either c or a.
>
> If c then s.
>
> If a then l.
>
> Therefore, either s or l.

A further argument in dilemma form could conclude, even more simply, something like "Either way we'll be unhappy." I'll leave this one to you to write out formally.

Since this is such a jolly little conclusion, maybe I should add that hedgehogs are actually quite able to get close without poking each other. They can be together and comfortable too. So Schopenhauer's second premise turns out to be false—at least for hedgehogs.

27

Reductio ad absurdum

One traditional deductive strategy deserves special mention even though, strictly speaking, it is only a version of *modus tollens*. This is the *reductio ad absurdum*, that is, a "reduction to absurdity." Arguments by *reductio* (or "indirect proof," as they're sometimes called) establish their conclusions by showing that assuming the opposite leads to absurdity: to a contradictory or silly result. Nothing is left to do, the argument suggests, but to accept the conclusion.

To prove: **p**.

Assume the opposite: Not-**p**.

Argue that from the assumption we'd have to conclude: **q**.

Show that **q** *is false (contradictory, "absurd," morally or practically unacceptable . . .).*

Conclude: **p** *must be true after all.*

Consider this intriguing little argument, for example:

> No one has yet had sex in space. No one has admitted to it, of course. But suppose, just for the sake of argument, that some-one who has been to space *did* have sex there. That would mean that someone who has had sex in space hasn't told any-one about it. And that is really hard to believe. No one would keep that to themselves![7]

Spelled out in *reductio* form, the argument is:

To prove: No one has yet had sex in space.

Assume the opposite: Someone *has* had sex in space.

Argue that from the assumption we'd have to conclude: Someone who has had sex in space has kept it secret.

But: That is "really hard to believe."

Conclude: No one has yet had sex in space.

A valid argument, but is the key premise true? Well, could *you* keep that secret?

---

7. Adapted by David Morrow from Mike Wall, "No Sex in Space Yet, Official Says," 22 April 2011. http://www.space.com/11473-astronauts-sex-space-rumors.html

28 Deductive arguments in multiple steps

Many valid deductive arguments are combinations of the basic forms introduced in Rules 22–27. Here, for example, is Sherlock Holmes performing a simple deduction for Doctor Watson's edification, meanwhile commenting on the relative roles of observation and deduction. Holmes has casually remarked that Watson visited a certain post office that morning, and furthermore that he sent off a telegram while there. "Right!" replies Watson, amazed, "Right on both points! But I confess that I don't see how you arrived at it." Holmes replies:

> "It is simplicity itself. . . . Observation tells me that you have a little reddish mold adhering to your instep. Just opposite the Wigmore Street Post Office they have taken up the pavement and thrown up some earth, which lies in such a way that it is difficult to avoid treading in it in entering. The earth is of this peculiar reddish tint which is found, as far as I know, nowhere else in the neighborhood. So much is observation. The rest is deduction."

> [Watson]: "How, then, did you deduce the telegram?"

> [Holmes]: "Why, of course I knew that you had not written a letter, since I sat opposite to you all morning. I see also in your open desk there that you have a sheet of stamps and a thick bundle of postcards. What could you go into the post office for, then, but to send a wire? Eliminate all other factors, and the one which remains must be the truth."[8]

Putting Holmes's deduction into explicit premises, we might have:

1. Watson has a little reddish mold on his boots.

2. If Watson has a little reddish mold on his boots, then he has been to the Wigmore Street Post Office this morning

---

8. Sir Arthur Conan Doyle, "The Sign of Four," in *The Complete Sherlock Holmes*, pp. 91–92.

(because there and only there is reddish dirt of that sort thrown up, and in a way difficult to avoid stepping in).

3. If Watson has been to the Wigmore Street Post Office this morning, he either mailed a letter, bought stamps or cards, or sent a wire.

4. If Watson had mailed a letter, he would have written the letter this morning.

5. Watson wrote no letter this morning.

6. If Watson had bought stamps or cards, he would not already have a drawer full of stamps and cards.

7. Watson already has a drawer full of stamps and cards.

8. Therefore, Watson sent a wire at the Wigmore Street Post Office this morning.

We now need to break the argument down into a series of valid arguments in the simple forms presented in Rules 22–27. We might start with a *modus ponens*:

2. If Watson has a little reddish mold on his boots, then he has been to the Wigmore Street Post Office this morning.

1. Watson has a little reddish mold on his boots.

I. Therefore, Watson has been to Wigmore Street Post Office this morning.

(I will use I, II, etc. to stand for the conclusions of simple arguments, which then can be used as premises to draw further conclusions.)
Another *modus ponens* follows:

3. If Watson has been to the Wigmore Street Post Office this morning, he either mailed a letter, bought stamps or cards, or sent a wire.

I. Watson has been to Wigmore Street Post Office this morning.

II. Therefore, Watson either mailed a letter, bought stamps or cards, or sent a wire.

Two of these three possibilities now can be ruled out, both by *modus tollens*:

4. If Watson had gone to the post office to mail a letter, he would have written the letter this morning.

5. Watson wrote no letter this morning.

III. Therefore, Watson did not go to the post office to mail a letter.

and

6. If Watson had gone to the post office to buy stamps or cards, he would not already have a drawer full of stamps and cards.

7. Watson already has a drawer full of stamps and cards.

IV. Therefore, Watson did not go to the post office to buy stamps or cards.

Finally we can put it all together:

II. Watson either mailed a letter, bought stamps or cards, or sent a wire at the Wigmore Street Post Office this morning.

III. Watson did not mail a letter.

IV. Watson did not buy stamps or cards.

8. Therefore, Watson sent a wire at the Wigmore Street Post Office this morning.

This last inference is an extended disjunctive syllogism: "Eliminate all other factors, and the one which remains must be the truth."

VII

Extended Arguments

Now suppose that you have picked, or been assigned, an issue or question on which to work out an argumentative essay or oral presentation. Maybe you're writing for a class; maybe you're about to speak at a public forum or write a Letter to the Editor; maybe you're just fascinated by the issue and want to figure out what you think.

To do this you need to go beyond the short arguments we have so far considered. You must work out a more detailed line of thought, in which the main ideas are laid out clearly and their own premises in turn are spelled out and defended. Anything you say requires evidence and reasons, which in turn may take some research, and you will need to weigh arguments for opposing views as well. All of this is hard work, but it is also good work. For many people, in fact, it is one of the most rewarding and enjoyable kinds of thinking there is!

29 Explore the issue

You begin with an issue but not necessarily a position. Do not feel that you must immediately embrace some position and then try to shore it up with arguments. Likewise, even if you have a position, do not just dash off the first argument that occurs to you. You are not being asked for the first opinion that occurs to you. You are being asked to *arrive* at a well-informed opinion that you can defend with solid arguments.

Is life likely on other planets? Here is one line of thought that some astronomers suggest. We are discovering that most stars have solar systems of their own. But there are hundreds of billions of stars in our galaxy alone—and hundreds of billions of galaxies in the universe. If even a tiny fraction of those billions and billions of solar systems have planets suitable for life, and even a tiny fraction of *those* actually *have* life, still there must be a myriad of planets with life. The number of chances would still be unimaginably huge.[9]

Then again, why do some people have doubts? Find out. Some scientists point out that we really have no idea how common habitable planets might be, or how likely life is to develop on them. It's all guesswork. Other critics argue that life elsewhere (or rather, intelligent life) by now should have announced itself, which (they say) hasn't happened.

All of these arguments carry some weight, and clearly much more must be said. You already see, then, that unexpected facts or perspectives may well turn up as you research and develop your argument. Be ready to be surprised. Be ready to hear evidence and arguments for positions you may not like. Be ready, even, to let yourself be swayed. True thinking is an open-ended process. The whole point is that you don't know when you start where you'll find yourself in the end.

Even if you have been assigned not just a topic but a position on that topic, you still need to look at arguments for a variety of other views—if only to be prepared to respond to them—and very likely you still have a lot of leeway about how to develop and defend the view you're given. On the most contentious issues, for example, you do not need to roll out the same arguments that everyone has heard a thousand times already. In fact, please don't! Look for creative new approaches. You could even try to find common ground with the other side. In short, take the time to choose your direction carefully, and aim to make some real progress on the issue, even (if you must) from within "given" positions.

---

9. For a contemporary presentation of this argument, see astronomer Seth Shostak, "Are We Alone?" in *Civilizations Beyond Earth*, edited by Douglas Vakoch and Albert Harrison (Berghahn, 2013), pp. 31–42.

30 Spell out basic ideas as arguments

Now remember that you are constructing *arguments*: that is, specific conclusions backed by evidence and reasons. As you begin to formulate a position, take its basic idea and frame it as an argument. Get out a large sheet of scratch paper and literally draft your premises and conclusion in outline.

Aim first for a relatively short argument—say, three to five premises—using the forms offered in this book. The basic argument just introduced for life on other planets, for example, might be put into premises-and-conclusion form in this way:

> There are many solar systems beyond our own.
>
> If there are many solar systems beyond our own, then it is very probable that there are other planets like Earth.
>
> If it is very probable that there are other planets like Earth, then it is very probable that some of them have life.
>
> Therefore, it is very probable that some other planets have life.

For practice, work this argument out as a deductive argument using *modus ponens* and hypothetical syllogism.

For another example, consider a quite different topic. Some people have recently proposed a major expansion of student exchange programs. Many more young Americans should have the chance to go abroad, they say, and many more young people from other parts of the world should have the chance to come here. It would cost money, of course, and would take some adjustment all around, but a more cooperative and peaceful world might result.

Suppose you want to develop and defend this proposal. First, again, sketch out the main argument for it—the basic idea. Why would people propose (and be so passionate about) expanding student exchange programs?

FIRST TRY:

Students who travel abroad learn to appreciate different countries.

More appreciation between different countries would be good.

Therefore, we should send more students abroad.

This outline does capture a basic idea, but in truth it is a little *too* basic. It hardly says enough to be much more than a simple assertion. Why, for example, would more appreciation between different countries be good? And how does sending students abroad produce it? Even a basic argument can be worked out a little further.

BETTER:

Students who travel abroad learn to appreciate other countries.

Students who travel abroad become person-to-person ambassadors who help their hosts appreciate the students' home countries.

More appreciation both ways will help us better coexist and cooperate in our interdependent world.

Therefore, we should send more students abroad.

You may have to try several different conclusions—even quite varied conclusions—before you find your best basic argument on a topic. Even after you have settled on the conclusion you want to defend, you may have to try several forms of argument before you find a form that really works well. (I am serious about that *large* sheet of scratch paper!) Again, use the rules in the earlier chapters of this book. Take your time—and give yourself time to take.

31

Defend basic premises with arguments of their own

Once you have spelled out your basic idea as an argument, it will need defense and development. For anyone who disagrees—in fact, for anyone who doesn't know much about the question in the first place—most of the basic premises will need supporting arguments of their own. Each premise therefore becomes the conclusion of a further argument that you need to work out.

Look back, for example, at the argument about life on other planets (p. 53). The argument begins with the premise that there are many solar systems beyond our own. This you can show by citing the scientific literature and news reports.

> As of 17 February 2017, the Paris Observatory's "Extrasolar Planet Encyclopaedia" lists 3,577 known planets of other stars, including many in multi-planet systems (http://exo planet.eu/).
>
> Therefore, there are many solar systems beyond our own.

The second premise of the basic argument for life on other planets is that *if* there are other solar systems beyond our own, then it is very probable that some of them include planets like Earth. Well, how do we know this? What's the supporting argument? Here you probably need to draw on factual knowledge and/or research. If you've paid attention to those same news reports, you have some good reasons to offer. The usual argument is an analogy:

> Our own solar system has a variety of kinds of planets, from gas giants to smaller rocky and watery planets suitable for life.
>
> As far as we know, other solar systems will be *like* ours.
>
> Therefore, if there are other solar systems beyond our own, then it is very probable that there are other planets like Earth.

Continue in this way for all the premises of your basic argument. Once again, it may take some work to find appropriate evidence for each premise that needs defense, and you may even find yourself changing some premises, and therefore the basic argument itself, so that they can be adequately supported by the kinds of evidence you end up finding. This is as it should be! Good arguments are usually in "flow," and each part depends on the others. It's a learning experience.

You'd need to approach the basic argument for student exchange programs in the same way. Why do you think, for instance—and how will you persuade others—that students who go abroad learn to appreciate other cultures? Examples would help, including perhaps the results of surveys or studies you can find through research or by consulting the experts (people who actually run student exchange programs, or social scientists). Again, in some way or other, you need to fill in the argument. The same goes for the second basic premise: how do we know that students abroad really do become "person-to-person ambassadors"?

The third basic premise (the value of mutual appreciation) is less likely to be confusing or contested, and in some quick arguments you could reasonably leave it undeveloped. (A point to remember: not *every* premise of your basic argument necessarily needs development and defense.) However, it is also a fine occasion to make the force of the argument—the expected benefits—more vivid. Maybe this way:

> Appreciation leads us to see virtues in others' ways, and to expect virtues even when we don't see them yet.

> Appreciation is also a form of enjoyment: it enriches our own experience.

> When we see or expect virtues in others' ways, and find that they enrich our own experience, we are less tempted to make harsh or single-minded judgments about them, and we will be better able to coexist and cooperate in our interdependent world.

> Therefore, mutual appreciation will help us better coexist and cooperate in our interdependent world.

Add some concrete examples to fill out these premises in turn, and you'll have yourself a fine argument overall.

32

Reckon with objections

Too often, when we make arguments, we concern ourselves only with the *pro* side: what can be said in support. Objections tend to come as a shock. We realize, maybe a little late, that we didn't think enough about possible problems. It's better to do so yourself and to hone your argument—maybe even make fundamental changes—in advance. In this way, you also make it clear to your eventual audience that you have done your homework, that you have explored the issue thoroughly and (hopefully!) with a somewhat open mind. So always ask: What are the best arguments *against* the conclusion you are working on?

Most actions have *many* effects, not just one. Maybe some of the other effects—ones you haven't looked at yet—are less desirable. Thoughtful and well-meaning people may oppose even such obviously good ideas ("obvious" to us, anyway) as eating more beans or getting married in order to be happy or sending more students abroad. Try to anticipate and honestly consider their concerns.

Students abroad, for example, may also end up in dangerous situations, and bringing large numbers of new foreign students here might raise national security risks. And all of it might cost a lot of money. These are important objections. On the other hand, perhaps they can be answered. Maybe you'll want to argue that the costs are worth it, for example, in part because there are also costs of *not* reaching out to other cultures. After all, we are already sending large numbers of young people—in the military—into extreme danger abroad. You could argue that giving ourselves another kind of face abroad might be a very good investment.

Other objections may lead you to rethink your proposal or argument. In this case, for example, worries about national security might require us to be careful about who is invited to come here. Clearly they need to come—how else are we going to correct false impressions?—but (you could argue) it could be fair to impose certain restrictions too.

Maybe you are making some general or philosophical claim: that humans have (or don't have) free will, for example, or that war is (or isn't) inherent in human nature, or that there is (or isn't) life on other planets. Here too, anticipate objections. If you are writing an academic paper, look for criticisms of your claim or interpretation in the class readings, secondary texts, or (good) online sources. Talk to people who have different views. Sift through the concerns and objections that come up, pick the strongest and most common ones, and try to answer them. And don't forget to re-evaluate your own argument. Do your premises or conclusion need to be changed or developed to take account of the objections?

33 Explore alternatives

If you are defending a proposal, it is not enough to show that your proposal will solve a problem. You must also show that it is better than other plausible ways of solving that same problem.

> Durham's swimming pools are overcrowded, especially on weekends. Therefore, Durham needs to build more pools.

This argument is weak in several ways. "Overcrowded" is vague, for one thing: who decides when there are too many people in a pool? Some people may even go for the crowds. But remedying this weakness still will not justify the conclusion. There may be other and more reasonable ways to address the (possible) problem.

Maybe the existing pools could have more open-swim hours so that swimmers could spread themselves over more available times. Maybe the typically lighter-use times could be more widely publicized. Maybe swim meets and other closed-pool activities could be moved to the weekdays. Or maybe Durham should do nothing at all and let users adjust their swim schedules for themselves. If you still want to argue that Durham should build more pools, you must show that your proposal is better than any of these (far less expensive) alternatives.

Exploring alternatives is not just a formality. The point is not just to quickly survey a few boringly obvious, easily countered alternatives and then (big surprise) to re-embrace your original proposal. Look for serious alternatives, and get creative. You might even come up with something quite new. How about . . . maybe keeping the pools open 24/7? How about putting in an evening smoothie bar or the like and enticing some of the day swimmers to come at odd hours instead?

If you come up with something really good, you might even need to change your conclusion. Are there possibly much better ways to organize foreign exchange programs, for instance? Maybe we should extend such opportunities to all sorts of people, not just students. How about exchange programs for *elders*? Why not for families, congregations, or work groups? Then it's not just about "sending students abroad" anymore . . . so it's back to your scratch paper to recast the basic argument. This is how real thinking works.

Even general or philosophical claims have alternatives. Some people argue, for instance, that there are not likely to be other civilizations elsewhere in the universe, because if there were, surely we'd have heard from them by now. But is the premise true? Aren't there other possibilities? Maybe other civilizations *are* out there, but are just listening. Maybe they choose to keep still, or just aren't interested, or are "civilized" in some other direction and do not have the technology. Maybe they are trying to communicate but not in the ways we are listening for. It's a very speculative question, but the existence of alternative possibilities like these does weaken the objection.

Many scientists also think, by the way, that life could arise on planets very different from Earth—it would just be a very different form of life. This is an alternative possibility too, and difficult to judge, but one that you could use to support and even extend the basic argument. Suppose life could be even more widespread than the basic argument suggests?

VIII

Argumentative Essays

Suppose now that you have explored your issue, outlined a basic argument, and defended its premises. You are ready to go public—maybe by writing an argumentative essay.

Remember that writing an extended argument is the *last* stage! If you have just picked up this book and opened it to this chapter, reflect: there is a reason that this is the eighth chapter and not the first. As the proverbial country Irishman said when a tourist asked him how to get to Dublin, "If you want to get to Dublin, don't start here."

Remember too that the rules in Chapters I–VI apply to writing an essay as well as to writing short arguments. Review the rules in Chapter I in particular. Be concrete and concise, build on substance and not overtone, and so forth. What follow are some additional rules specific to writing argumentative essays.

34 Jump right in

Launch straight into the real work. No windy windups or rhetorical padding.

NO:

> For centuries, philosophers have debated the best way to be happy. . . .

We knew that already. Get to *your* point.

YES:

> In this essay I will try to show that the best things in life really *are* free.

35 Urge a definite claim or proposal

If you are making a proposal, be specific. "Something should be done" is not a real proposal. You need not be elaborate. "Cell phones should be banned while driving" is a specific proposal but also a very simple one. If you want to argue that the United States should expand study-abroad programs, though, the idea is more complex and therefore needs some elaboration.

Similarly, if you are making a philosophical claim or defending your interpretation of a text or event, begin by stating your claim or interpretation *simply*.

> Very probably there is life on other planets.

That's forthright and clear!

Academic essays may aim simply to assess some of the arguments for or against a claim or proposal. You may not be making a claim or proposal of your own or even arriving at a specific decision. For example, you may be able to examine only one line of argument in a controversy. If so, make it clear immediately that this is what you are doing. Sometimes your conclusion may be simply that the arguments for or against some position or proposal are inconclusive. Fine—but make that conclusion clear immediately. You don't want your own essay to seem inconclusive!

36

Your argument is your outline

You now move to the main body of your essay: your argument. First, just summarize it. Take the basic argument you've outlined and put it into a concise paragraph.

> Many solar systems are now being discovered beyond our own. I will argue that many of them are likely to include planets like Earth. Many of these planets in turn are likely to have life. Very probably, then, there is life on other planets.

Here your aim is just to give the reader the big picture: a clear overview of where you are going and how you propose to get there.

An argumentative essay should now advance each of the premises of this basic argument in turn, each with a paragraph that begins with a restatement of the premise and continues by developing and defending it.

> Consider first the remarkable fact that many other solar systems are being discovered beyond our own. As of 17 February 2017, the Paris Observatory's "Extrasolar Planet Encyclopaedia" lists 3,577 known planets of other stars, including many in multi-planet systems (http://exoplanet.eu/). . . .

You might go on to discuss a few examples—say, the most recent and intriguing discoveries. In a longer essay, you might cite other lists too, and/or explain the methods being used to discover these planets—it depends on how much room you have and the level of detail and support your readers need or expect. Then go on to explain and defend your other basic premises in the same way.

Some premises in your basic argument may need fairly involved defenses. Treat them exactly the same way. First state the premise you are defending and remind your readers of its role in your main argument. Next summarize your argument for that premise in turn (that is, treating it now as the conclusion of a further argument). Then spell out that argument, giving a paragraph or so, in order, to each of *its* premises.

For instance, in the last chapter (Rule 31) we developed a defense of the second premise of the basic argument for life on other planets. You could insert it now in paragraph form and with a little more style.

> Why might we think that other solar systems include planets like Earth? Astronomers propose an intriguing argument by analogy. They point out that our own solar system has a variety of kinds of planets—some huge gas giants, some others rocky and well suited for liquid water and life. As far as we know, they continue, other solar systems will be *like* ours. Therefore, they conclude, other solar systems very probably contain a variety of planets, including some that are rocky and well suited for liquid water and life.

Now you may need to explain and defend these points in turn, maybe even giving some of them their own paragraph or two each. You could try to awaken your readers' appreciation for the diversity of planets right here in our solar system, for example, or describe some of the variety of extra-solar planets already known.

Depending on how long and involved all of this gets, you may need to reorient your reader to the basic argument when you return to it. Pull out the road map, as it were, and remind your readers—and yourself—where you are in your journey toward the main conclusion.

> We have seen, then, that solar systems are already being discovered beyond our own, and that it seems very probable that there are other planets like Earth. The last main premise of the argument is this: if there are other planets like Earth, then very probably some of them have life.

In your outline you will have worked out an argument for this premise too, and you can now bring it smoothly up to bat.

Notice, in all of these arguments, the importance of using consistent terms (Rule 6). Clearly connected premises such as these become the parallel sentences or phrases that hold the whole essay together.

37

Detail objections and meet them

Rule 32 asks you to think about and rework your argument in light of possible objections. Detailing and responding to them in your essay helps to make your views more persuasive to your readers, and attests that you have thought carefully about the issue.

NO:

> Someone might object that expanded student exchange programs will create too many risks for students. But *I* think that . . .

Well, what kinds of risks? Why would such risks arise? Spell out the *reasons* behind the objection. Take the time to sketch the whole counter-argument, not just to mention its conclusion as you rush by to defend *your* argument.

YES:

> Someone might object that expanded student exchange programs will create too many risks for students. The concern is partly, I think, that students abroad, who are mostly young people, after all, and not so worldly, may be more easily taken advantage of or hurt, especially in places where life is more desperate and there are fewer safeguards and protections.
>
> In this time of rising fear and mistrust of foreigners, coupled with fears of terrorism, the concern may also take on more of an edge: students' lives may be at stake. We would certainly not want exchange students to become hostages in desperate local power games. Western tourists abroad are already sometimes targeted by terrorists; we could justifiably fear that the same might happen to exchange students.
>
> These are serious concerns. Still, equally serious responses are also possible. . . .

Now it is clear exactly what the objections are, and you can try to respond to them effectively. You might point out, for instance, that risks don't just start at the border. Many foreign countries are safer than many American cities. A more complex response might be that it is also risky, at least to our society as a whole, *not* to send more cultural ambassadors abroad, since international misunderstandings and the hatreds they fuel are making the world more risky for all of us.

And surely there are creative ways to design exchange programs to reduce some of the risks? You might not even have thought of these possibilities, though, if you had not detailed the arguments behind the objection, and your readers would probably not have seen the point even if you had mentioned them. Detailing the objections enriches *your* argument in the end.

38 Seek feedback and use it

Maybe you know exactly what you mean. Everything seems clear to you. However, it may be far from clear to anyone else! Points that seem connected to you may seem completely unrelated to someone reading your essay. I have seen students hand in an essay that they think is sharp and clear only to find, when they get it back, that they themselves can barely understand what they were thinking when they wrote it. Their grades won't be very encouraging either.

Writers—at all levels—need *feedback*. It is through others' eyes that you can see best where you are unclear or hasty or just plain implausible. Feedback improves your logic too. Objections may come up that you hadn't expected. Premises you thought were secure may turn out to need defending, while other premises may turn out to be more secure than they seemed. You may even pick up a few new facts or examples. Feedback is a "reality check" all the way around. Welcome it.

Some teachers build student feedback on paper drafts right into the timetable of their classes. If your teacher does not, arrange it yourself. Find willing fellow students and exchange drafts. Go to your campus Writing Center (yes, you have one). Encourage your readers to be critical, and commit yourself to being a critical reader for them in turn. If need be, you might even assign your readers a quota of specific criticisms and suggestions to make, so they don't fear hurting your feelings by suggesting some. It may be polite, but it really does *not* do you a favor if your would-be critics just glance over your writing and reassure you that it is lovely, whatever it says. Your teacher and eventual audience will not give you such a free pass.

We may underrate feedback partly because we typically don't see it at work. When we only read finished pieces of writing—essays, books, magazines—it can be easy to miss the fact that writing is essentially a *process*. The truth is that every single piece of writing you read is put together by someone who starts from scratch and makes hundreds of choices and multiple revisions along the way. This very book you hold in your hands has gone through at least twenty drafts throughout its five editions, with formal and informal feedback from dozens and dozens of people. Development, criticism, clarification, and change are the keys. Feedback is what makes them go.

Modesty, please!

Summarize at the end—fairly. Don't claim more than you've shown.

NO:

> In sum, every reason favors sending more students abroad, and none of the objections stands up at all. What are we waiting for?

YES:

> In sum, there is an appealing case for sending more students abroad. Although uncertainties may remain, on the whole it seems to be a promising step. It's worth a try.

Maybe the second version overdoes it in the other direction, but you see the point. Very seldom will you put all the objections to rest, and anyway the world is an uncertain place. We're not experts, most of us, and even the experts can be wrong. "It's worth a try" is the best attitude.

IX

Oral Arguments

Sometimes you will find yourself arguing out loud: debating in front of a class; arguing for a bigger share of the student government budget or speaking for your neighborhood at City Council; invited to make a presentation on a subject of your interest or expertise by a group that is interested. Sometimes your audience will be friendly, sometimes they will be neutral but willing to listen, and sometimes they will really need to be won over. At all times, you'll want to present good arguments effectively.

All of the rules in the earlier chapters of this book apply to oral arguments as well as argumentative essays. Here are a few further rules for oral arguments in particular.

40 Ask for a hearing

In making an oral argument you are quite literally asking for a *hearing*. You want to be heard: to be listened to with respect and at least some degree of open-mindedness. But your hearers may or may not start out respectful or open-minded, and may not even bring a genuine interest in your topic. You need to reach out to them to create the kind of hearing you want to have.

One way to reach out is through your own enthusiasm. Bring some of your own interest and energy for the topic into your talk early on. It personalizes you and notches up the energy in the room.

> I appreciate the chance to speak to you today. In this talk, I want to put forward a new idea on the subject of student exchange programs. It's a proposal I find exciting and inspiring, and I'm hoping that, by the end, you will too.

Notice also that this way of talking itself displays the inviting attitude toward your hearers that you'd like them to take toward you. You may not get it back from them, even so—but you certainly won't get it from them if you don't bring it to them in the first place. Arguing face to face can be a powerful thing, and done deftly and persistently, it can reinforce and build respect itself, even across major differences.

Never give an audience the feeling that you are talking down to them. They may know less than you do about the subject, but they can certainly learn, and it is pretty likely that you have some learning to do too. You're not there to rescue them from their ignorance, but rather to share some new information or ideas that you hope they'll find as intriguing and suggestive as you do. Again, approach your audience from *enthusiasm*, not some sort of superiority.

Respect your audience, then, and also respect yourself. You are there because you have something to offer, and they are there either because they want to hear it or because it is required by their jobs or studies. You do not need to apologize for taking their time. Just thank them for listening, and use the time well.

41 Be fully present

A public talk or speech is a face-to-face occasion. It is not simply a public version of what we do privately when we read. After all, if people just wanted your words, reading would be much more efficient. They are there partly for your *presence*.

So, be present! For starters, look at your audience. Take the time to connect. Meet people's eyes and hold them. People who get nervous speaking to groups are sometimes advised to talk to one person in the group, as if one to one. Do so, if you need to, but then go a step further: talk to your whole audience one to one, one person at a time.

Speak with expression. Do not read your pre-prepared words as if it were a chore. Remember, you're *talking* to people here! Imagine that you are having an animated conversation with a friend (OK, maybe a little one-sided . . .). Now speak to your audience in the same spirit.

Writers seldom get to see their readers. When you speak in public, though, your hearers are right there in front of you, and you have constant feedback from them. Use it. Do people meet your eyes with interest? What is the feeling in the audience as a whole? Are people leaning forward to hear better . . . or not? If not, can you pick up the energy? Even if you have a presentation to get through, you can still adjust your style, or stop to explain or review a key point if necessary. When you are not sure of your audience, plan in advance to be able to adjust to different responses. Have an extra story or illustration ready to go, just in case.

By the way, you are not glued to the floor behind the podium (should you have one). You can walk around or at least come out from behind the lectern. Depending on your own comfort level and the occasion, you can establish a much more engaged feeling in the room by visibly engaging with your audience yourself.

42 Signpost energetically

Readers can take in an argument selectively. They can stop and think, double back, or choose to drop it entirely and move on to something else. Your listeners can't do any of these things. You set the pace for everyone.

So be considerate. On the whole, oral arguments need to offer more signposting and repetition than written arguments. At the beginning, you may need to summarize the argument more fully, and then you need to refer more regularly back to the summary, or what Rule 36 called the "roadmap." For your summary, use labels like "Here is my basic argument." For your premises, as the argument turns, say something like, "We come now to the second [third, fourth, etc.] basic premise of my argument. . . ." Summarize again at the end. Pause to mark important transitions and to give people time to think.

In my college debate training I was taught to literally repeat my key claims word for word—that's right, to literally repeat my key claims word for word—mainly because other people were writing them down. Sometimes I still do this as a teacher: it shows that you know that people are listening hard and that they may want or need the key points signposted. In other settings, this might seem odd. Even if you don't repeat the key points word for word, at least mark them out in some way, and make it clear that—and why—you are doing so.

Be especially alert to your audience at important transitions. Look around and make sure that most of your hearers are ready to move with you. You'll communicate better and show your audience that you actually care that they take in and understand what you are saying.

43 Hew your visuals to your argument

Some visuals may help your presentation. Maybe your argument is complex enough that just seeing it written out can help your hearers. So hand out an outline. If you are presenting it in parts, slides can highlight the various parts as you move to them— an effective way to signpost. Or your argument may depend on certain kinds of data or other information that a few slides can illustrate. Maybe a short video can illustrate a key point or bring other compelling voices briefly into your case.

But go light on these visuals. Don't just turn yourself into a slide-reader: your audience can do that better, and certainly faster, than you can. Meanwhile the bells and whistles in many visual presentation programs turn into major distractions in their own rights. And PowerPoint, the old standard, at this point is (let's face it) pretty boring. Critics have also pointed out that cramming ideas into slide formats tends to oversimplify. The text on slides typically is very clipped; charts and graphs can display little detail. And the inevitable technical glitches during presentations lead to distractions and sometimes total disaster.

To "hew" means to cut something back and shape it to fit. Rule 43 uses the term quite deliberately. Remember: your *argument* is the key thing. Cut and shape your use of visuals accordingly. Consider also whether your argument would be better developed, or your audience better engaged with it, in some quite different way. Ask for a show of hands on some subject, perhaps, or solicit some structured audience participation. Read briefly from a book or article. Put up a short video clip or some graphs or data, if needed, but then turn the screen off to continue talking.

For the display of information, consider paper handouts. You can include far more—complex words and pictures; graphs, data, references, links—including much that can be left for people to read before or after the presentation if they choose. Distribute your handouts in advance, or only when you are ready to use them, or for reference at the end—and encourage people to take them when they go.

44 End in style

First of all, end on time. Find out how long you are supposed to speak and don't go over. You know from your own experiences as a listener that nothing irritates an audience more than a speaker who goes on too long.

But don't just peter out. You don't want to conclude by simply turning out the lights.

NO:

> Well, I guess that's about all the time I have. Why don't I stop and we can chat a bit if any of these ideas have interested you?

Come to a rousing end. End on a high note—with flair or a flourish.

YES:

> In this talk I have tried to suggest that real happiness is attainable after all, and by everyone; that it takes no special luck or wealth; indeed, that its preconditions lie within easy reach, all around us. I thank you for your attention, my friends, and naturally wish you all the greatest happiness yourselves!

X

Public Debates

A public debate may be a face-to-face conversation between people who care about a topic but come to it with very different points of view. Or it may be a larger occasion—more people involved, more points of view—in a classroom or community meeting. It may be a version of the political debates we sometimes see in public forums or on television. Or it may be carried on slower motion, through the exchange of extended written arguments—editorials, speeches, and the like—like those you have practiced constructing in Chapter VIII.

Today most people would probably say that we are getting worse at this: that public argument, and especially political argument, is growing more shrill, less rational, more destructive than constructive. I am not sure that this is entirely true: it may just be that we romanticize the past. Still, it is certainly true that we can do a lot better. Here are some rules that should help.

45 Do argument proud

In public debate, as in any other kind of argument, give it your best. Today, especially, public debate is not easy. Stakes are high, shared solid ground seems hard to find, and passions are inflamed. On the other hand, you could also think: these are the kinds of times that argument has been waiting for. This is why you have rules for arguments in this book and have worked to build your skill at using them. So, use them! Seek the best evidence; don't overgeneralize; take care with statistics; use analogies that are illuminating and relevant. Use only the best sources. Detail objections and try to meet them . . . and all the rest.

The invitation is not simply to "sound off." Public debate is not another kind of opinion polling, and—as this book has tried to show from the start—argument of any kind is not simply a kind of fight. Public debate is, ideally, a process of *thinking together.* Come ready to do so. Join a debate to which you can genuinely contribute. Enter it with something worth arguing about. Bring some genuine evidence and ideas, and use your skills to present them fairly and well.

And for sure, bring your passions. Many arguments arise from our passions and articulate and ground them—especially in challenging times. The critical point is only that passion is not an argument by itself. That someone feels strongly about some claim does not, by itself, give us a good reason to believe it. That a claim is made more insistently or shrilly does not make it better—in fact, you may begin to wonder whether the sound and fury are a cover for a lack of evidence. A good argument *justifies* its passion!

46 Listen, learn, leverage

Debate is an *exchange.* It is a back-and-forth with other people holding other positions, with their own arguments that they are also (ideally) trying to make as well as possible. It is not simply an occasion for you to declare your own position—nor is it an occasion for other people to simply declare theirs. Both you and they need to *listen* to each other.

NO:

> I can't think of anything stupider than giving up meat. People have always eaten it. Besides, our teeth aren't made just for chewing beans!

Although this sounds a lot like how some debates tend to go, it is exactly the wrong way to start. Someone who really can't think of anything stupider than such a widely held position probably just doesn't understand it at all (really? you can't think of *anything* more stupid?). Throwing in a few one-line reasons to cover for

dismissing the entire position without even considering its arguments is an unwise move too. (Dental capacity is destiny, eh?)

Try for a more open-minded approach—before you "come back"
with your own views. Your job is not only to understand other debaters' conclusions, but also to understand their premises, their
reasons—to listen for their *arguments*. This means much more than
passively waiting out someone's statement of their views. You need to
actively seek out their reasons, and understand why they find those
reasons so compelling.

YES:

> I am still trying to understand people who think we should
> give up meat. How can some people go so far as to give up a
> type of food humans have always eaten? And aren't our di-
> gestive systems meant partly for meat?

The "No" statement is a declaration and a dismissal. There is nowhere to go from it—at least not without jumping right into a fight.
But the "Yes" statement is a set of questions. You are still unper-
suaded, but this time you clearly signal your wish to understand the
other argument(s), and leave some space for your own rethinking
too. Maybe you can even help out their argument a little bit too. At
least, you will probably learn something, and in any case you'll be
better prepared to advance your own argument when your turn
comes.

Your turn—yes. For this little exchange is by no means over.

Suppose that you have listened actively and questioned carefully,
to the full satisfaction of the person you are arguing with. You have
worked hard to understand their argument. Now you are entitled to
ask for the same careful, extended, and active listening back. You
have some *leverage*.

> Thank you for taking the time to explore your argument with
> me. I know I had lots of questions—we have talked about
> some interesting answers. I will have to think more about it.
> Now I'd like to explain *my* argument to *you*. Please ask ques-
> tions as we go along, too. Ready?

Some debaters will be surprised at this, even caught out. So far it has been all about them and their arguments. It's gratifying—and rare—to be listened to so well in public arguments (or anywhere, for that matter). They may even think that because you have carefully worked through their argument with them, you now agree with them (which you might, of course, but not necessarily).

Now, suddenly, they realize that the exchange is only half over. Now *they* have to listen, and in something like the open-minded way you have just modeled. This may be a new experience for many debaters. But they can hardly object, can they, since you have just listened so carefully and actively to *them?* So get on with it.

47 Offer something positive

Public debates often get stuck because the people involved can see no good way forward. In part this is because so much of the focus is relentlessly negative—on what's wrong with the other side. Better arguments offer people something to *affirm*—something appealing and positive.

Come to a debate, then, with some suggestions about a better direction forward. Build up your candidate or position, don't just tear down the other side. Propose some way to respond, something to do, not just something to resist or avoid or lament. Offer something real to do, something to hope for, some sense of possibility—at least some kind of positive spin.

NO:

> This city stinks at conserving water! Even with the reservoirs down to a month's supply, we've only been able to cut back consumption by 25 percent. And people still don't get it about not washing their cars or leaving their sprinklers going forever. . . .

Maybe, maybe . . . But when we focus on the severity of a problem, we also run the risk of making people feel like nothing can be done about it. Couldn't the same issue be framed in a more empowering way?

YES:

> This city can and must conserve more water. We've been able to cut back consumption by 25 percent so far, but with the reservoirs down to a month's supply, people should really start seeing the need to stop washing their cars or leaving their sprinklers going . . .

These are exactly the same facts, even stated in similar phrases and sentences, but the overall feeling is sharply different.

The point is not to be mindlessly optimistic. We should not ignore what is negative. But when we let it fill the screen entirely, negativity becomes the only reality. We create more of it, we preoccupy ourselves with it, and it gets our energy and attention, even if we wish to resist it.

Part of the power of Martin Luther King, Jr.'s iconic "I Have a Dream" speech is that it is, after all, about *dreams*: about visions for a shared and just future. "I have a dream that the children of former slaves and the children of former slave-owners will be able to sit down together at the table of brotherhood. . . ." Imagine if he'd spoken only about nightmares instead: "I have a *nightmare* that the children of former slaves and the children of former slave-owners will *never* be able to sit down together at the table of brotherhood. . . ." In one way this is exactly the same idea—but if King had put it this way, would his great speech live on today?

All arguments—not just in public debates—should try to offer something positive. Again, though, there is a special energy and often urgency in public debates, which is why I place this rule in this chapter. A group's optimism and excitement can be infectious, and it can become a power of its own, as can a sense of gloom and disempowerment. Which will you choose to create?

48

Work from common ground

Public debate is often framed by extreme positions. In fact, however, even most partisans in those debates actually hold "in-between" views when they speak more thoughtfully and carefully. Hardly anyone truly favors wholly eliminating guns, say, or ending all oil drilling. Likewise, hardly anyone favors leaving guns, or oil drilling, wholly unrestricted. Even in the never-ending and highly divisive abortion debate, most pro-choice advocates accept and indeed often favor *some* restrictions on abortion, and most pro-life advocates are willing to accept abortion in *some* circumstances.

You have to *look* for this kind of common ground. If you only expect bumper-sticker-positions, simple and insistent, not only will you will find them, but probably they're *all* you will find. Everything else—the nuance of even the fiercest positions, and all views between—will be pushed into the shadows. Advocates of in-between positions may themselves feel forced toward the extremes, in order to be heard at all.

When you look for in-between views and areas of overlap, disagreements—while still quite real—will seem manageable, even potentially productive.

> We still seem to differ about the causes of climate change. Whether it is mostly caused by natural processes or by human activity, though, surely we need to respond to it by smarter building and emergency planning. The seas are rising. Shouldn't we be working together to meet these new challenges, regardless of cause?

Even when disagreements really are radical, it is still more useful to try to work toward some sort of compromise, rather than trying to convert someone straight out. You may debate animal rights all day, but most people on both (all!) sides would probably at least agree that we would be better off if we ate *less* meat. Pro-life and pro-choice sides actually have wide areas of agreement and have even worked together at times, for example to reduce the felt need for abortion in the first place.[10] Disagreements certainly remain in these cases, and they are important and worth talking about, but they needn't fill the whole screen or claim all our energy. There are intelligent ways of making progress together.

Moreover, people's actual positions are usually complex and, well, just plain *interesting*—even those with which we may disagree. Gun advocates have legitimate concerns about citizens being defenseless against tyranny if guns are outlawed, while gun opponents have legitimate concerns about safety when guns are everywhere. Meanwhile the actual evidence tends to complicate things, as it often does. Many countries have strict gun control without any kind of tyranny—Canada, for example. Meanwhile, the United States has far more guns per capita than almost any other country, including the most war-torn, but also a comparatively moderate gun death *rate*, although the sheer number remains distressingly high. Seriously addressing facts like these might transform the gun debate into something quite different.

Still, there will be occasions where no change seems possible without repeated, persistent, even radical opposition. Go to it, then. But beware of supposing that *every* debate must be such a battle, or every argument a battering ram against the other side's perversity or ignorance. No matter how *they* approach *you*—at first—invite something more collaborative, as if you both stand on the same side and need to address a shared problem together. Stick to it until they get it. See what happens.

This approach might be used in more formal public debates too—debates with an audience, for example. Set it up not as two people versus each other, or even two arguments versus each other, but as a forum for *exploring* the arguments around an issue. And include more than two!

---

10. Google the Common Ground Network for Life and Choice, a project of Search for Common Ground, whose current projects also deserve a look. For an academic treatment, see Robin West, Justin Murray, and Meredith Esser, editors, *In Search of Common Ground: From Culture War to Reproductive Justice* (Ashgate, 2014).

49

At least be civil

Don't deride or attack other debaters. This is a mistake that even has its own name: the *ad hominem* ("to the man") fallacy (see Appendix I). You don't have to like the people you are debating with, let alone agree with them. You may have trouble even taking them seriously—and likely they will return the (dis)favor. You can still have some courtesy. So can they. In a way, such occasions are what civility is *for*.

Focus on their arguments. Describe your opponents' position in fair ways. Avoid loaded language: build on *substance*, as Rule 5 puts it, not overtone. Make it clear that you know that they have premises worth considering, even if you wholly reject their conclusions or their premises in the end.

> **NO:**
>
> My opponent's argument reeks of centuries of illiberal ideas, going all the way back to Plato's self-serving rationalization for the dictatorship of the elite. He ought to be ashamed to bring such discredited propaganda into public discussion today . . .

> **YES:**
>
> My opponent's argument stands in a long tradition of conservative political thinking, going all the way back to the Athenian philosopher Plato's mistrust of democracy. Plato had his reasons, for sure. That he was right, however, or that his reasons apply today, is quite another matter . . .

Think of it as a minimalist kind of ethics. For better or worse, everyone with whom you debate is still part of the same society, someone with whom you have to live at the end of the day, and moreover is probably not an absolute scoundrel or crazy either. We debate with real people, not with some stuffed-shirt caricatures. We're all trying to make sense of a world that is complex and constantly in flux, not comprehended fully by any of us. And we are all trying, by our arguments among other means, to improve things a little bit, at least as we see it. Even the ranters and the most closed-minded, however backwards they appear to us. Civility honors them at least for that.

And of course, likewise, we wish to be treated civilly ourselves, even by those who disagree with *us* and might even place *us*, shockingly enough, among the ranters or the closed-minded. From a purely practical point of view, then, civility gives us some leverage, as Rule 46 puts it. When we are civil to others, we have a clearer right to ask the same civility back. Certainly you are more apt to get civility back if you offer it than if you don't!

Sometimes it is hard to even think straight when we feel deliberately misrepresented and put down. In that case, you aren't likely to feel too generous to the other side when your turn comes. Just remember that your opponents feel the same way. Civility appeals to everyone's better selves.

Besides, maybe—just maybe—your opponents aren't totally wrong. In an uncertain and complex world, there is more than one way to "put it all together," as represented by the many people who *do* put it all together in ways very different from ourselves. We may have a few things to learn from them, or at least it would be polite to act as though we do. Civility in this case is partly a kind of honest humility.

You don't feel like others are being very civil right now? Me neither. We may hope for civility back from others, but we may not get it. Again, though, it is the job of civil debaters to get out in front regardless. Take the lead. Do it *first*. Maybe your generosity will be infectious, a model to others to shift their ways of debating too. In any case, you thereby uplift civility itself, in the larger society, even if it might have to follow a wider track to come back to you again.

Leave them thinking when you go

Even the best argument in the world is only part of a debate—maybe quite a small part. Debates stay with us because they have many related aspects, draw on many facts and claims that may be uncertain or controversial or conflicting themselves, and allow a variety of conclusions. Philosophers have been debating about happiness, for example, for a few thousand years. Certainly we have made progress, but no argument has simply "won," nor, surely, should it.

Single arguments may make a difference, then, but rarely will one argument make *all* the difference, even if it is completely correct. Single arguments or arguers may address one aspect of a debate, revise and improve certain other arguments, take up other aspects or new ideas . . . all the time changing as they go. But the debate itself shifts slowly, usually, like a great ship turning in the sea.

The upshot is that public debate takes patience. The great ship is going to turn slowly no matter how energetically or persuasively we hold forth on deck. And because it is whole debates that shift, carrying with them a jumble of specific arguments on all sides, people may not change their minds on the biggest themes even when they acknowledge unanswered arguments against some parts of their views. The world may still seem to make more sense the old way. And they are not being irrational, any more than you or I are being irrational in holding onto *our* own favorite views of things even when (to be honest) there may be good arguments against parts of them also. Change not only takes time, it usually takes a more attractive overall view of things too.

No matter how good your argument is, then, do not expect most people to rise as one to agree with you the moment you finish your case. Instead, just ask for their open-minded consideration. Expect them to be willing to *consider* changing. And, again, you will be most successful at this if you are visibly willing to consider changing yourself. Pushing harder may just bring up those unpleasant stereotypes of "argument" that drive people further into rigid thinking.

Debate is certainly not the only, or even always the best way of taking part in public discourse. There will be times when passionate appeals are more to the point, perhaps, or personal testimony, or sermons. Moreover, there may be times when we are sorely tempted to make bad arguments ourselves: knowingly using loaded language, dubious sources, and all the rest, especially when it seems like the other side stoops that low routinely. It's tempting, yes. But let me close with two cautions.

One: in the long run, making bad arguments devalues good arguments—careful thinking—in general. This cannot be good for our society. Unfortunately, at times, it might be your side that has to carry the burden of clarity and thoughtfulness, if the other side truly is not. Still, in the long run, standing up for good arguments is the only truly winning way.

Second, honestly, if the other side really does routinely stoop that low, then they are also probably much better at it: much better practiced, much better funded, and with many fewer remaining compunctions. It's not a winning game for you. Play instead to *your* strength—doing argument proud, now that you have this book under your belt—which happens to be the right thing to do as well.

Raise good arguments, then, as openly and thoughtfully as you can. Offer something positive. Hear the other side out, and respond and connect as best you can. But recognize that the debate will continue. Life is short, the debate is long. There are also many worthwhile and constructive things to do besides debate, both in and out of public discourse. At some point you will need to step away. Just leave them thinking when you go!

Appendix I

Some Common Fallacies

Fallacies are misleading types of arguments. Many of them are so tempting, and therefore so common, that they even have their own names. This may make them seem like a separate and new topic. Actually, though, to call something a fallacy is usually just another way of saying that it violates one of the rules for *good* arguments. The fallacy of "false cause," for example, is a questionable conclusion about causes, and you can look to Chapter V for explanation.

Here is a short list and explanation of some of the classical fallacies, including their Latin names when frequently used.

ad hominem (literally, "to the man"): attacking the *person* of a source rather than his or her qualifications or reliability or the actual argument he or she makes. You know from Chapter IV that supposed authorities may be disqualified if they are not informed, impartial, or largely in agreement. But other sorts of attacks on supposed authorities are typically not legitimate.

> It's no surprise that Carl Sagan argued for life on Mars—after all, he was a well-known atheist. I don't believe it for a minute.

Although Sagan did take part in the public discussion about religion and science, there is no reason to think that his views about religion colored his scientific judgment about Martian life. Look to the argument, not "the man."

ad ignorantiam (appeal to ignorance): arguing that a claim is true just because it has not been shown to be false. A classic example is this statement by Senator Joseph McCarthy when he was asked for evidence to back up his accusation that a certain person was a Communist:

> I do not have much information on this except the general statement of the agency that there is nothing in the files to disprove his Communist connections.

Of course, apparently there was nothing to *prove* it, either.

ad misericordiam (appeal to pity): appealing to pity as an argument for special treatment.

> I know I flunked every exam, but if I don't pass this course, I'll have to retake it in summer school. You *have* to let me pass!

Pity is sometimes a good reason to help, but it is certainly inappropriate when objective evaluation is called for.

ad populum: appealing to the emotions of a crowd; also, appealing to a person to go along with the crowd ("Everyone's doing it!"). Arguments *ad populum* are good examples of *bad* arguments from authority. No reasons are offered to show that "everybody" is any kind of knowledgeable or reliable source.

affirming the consequent: a deductive mistake of the form

> If **p** then **q**.
>
> **q**.
>
> Therefore, **p**.

Remember that in the statement "if **p** then **q**," **p** is called the "antecedent" and **q** the "consequent." The second premise of *modus ponens*—a valid form—affirms (asserts) the antecedent, **p** (go back to Rule 22 and check). Affirming the consequent (**q**), though, yields quite a different—and invalid—form. A true conclusion is not guaranteed even if the premises are true. For example:

> When the roads are icy, the mail is late.
>
> The mail is late.
>
> Therefore, the roads are icy.

Although the mail would be late if the roads were icy, it may be late for other reasons too. This argument **overlooks alternatives**.

begging the question: implicitly using your conclusion as a premise.

> God exists because it says so in the Bible, which I know is true because God wrote it, after all!

To put this argument in premise-and-conclusion form, you'd have to write:

> The Bible is true, because God wrote it.
>
> The Bible says that God exists.
>
> Therefore, God exists.

To defend the claim that the Bible is true, the arguer claims that God wrote it. But, obviously, if God wrote the Bible, then God exists. Thus the argument assumes just what it is trying to prove.

circular argument: same as **begging the question.**

> You can count on WARP News for the facts, because the station's motto is "we just give you the facts," so that must be a fact too!

Real-life circular arguments often follow a bigger circle, but they all eventually end up starting in the very place they want to end.

complex question: posing a question in such a way that people cannot agree *or* disagree with you without committing themselves to some other claim you wish to promote. A simple example: "Are you still as self-centered as you used to be?" Answering either "yes" or "no" commits you to agreeing that you used to be self-centered. A more subtle example: "Will you follow your conscience instead of your pocketbook and donate to the cause?" Saying "no," regardless of their real reasons for not donating, makes people feel guilty. Saying "yes," regardless of their real reasons for donating, makes them noble. If you want a donation, just ask for it.

denying the antecedent: a deductive mistake of the form

> If **p** then **q**.
>
> Not-**p**.
>
> Therefore, not-**q**.

Remember that, in the statement "If **p** then **q**," **p** is called the "antecedent" and **q** the "consequent." The second premise of a *modus tollens*—a valid form—denies the consequent, **q** (go back to Rule 23 and check). Denying the antecedent (**p**), though, yields quite a different—and invalid—form. A true conclusion is not guaranteed even if the premises are true. For example:

> When the roads are icy, the mail is late.
>
> The roads are not icy.
>
> Therefore, the mail is not late.

Although the mail would be late if the roads were icy, it may be late for other reasons too. This argument **overlooks alternatives.**

equivocation: sliding from one meaning of a term to another in the middle of an argument.

> Women and men are physically and emotionally different. The sexes are *not* "equal," then, and therefore the law should not pretend that we are.

Between premise and conclusion this argument shifts the meaning of the term "equal." The sexes are not physically and emotionally "equal" in the sense in which "equal" means simply "identical." Equality before the law, however, does not mean "physically and emotionally identical" but "entitled to the same rights and opportunities."

Rephrased with the two different senses of "equal" made clear, the argument goes:

> Women and men are not physically and emotionally identical. Therefore, women and men are not entitled to the same rights and opportunities.

Once the equivocation is removed, it is clear that the argument's conclusion is neither supported by nor even related to the premise. No reason is offered to show that physical and emotional differences imply different rights and opportunities.

false cause: generic term for any questionable conclusion about cause and effect. To figure out specifically *why* the conclusion is (said to be) questionable, go back to Chapter V.

false dilemma: reducing the options you consider to just two, often diametrically opposed to each other and unfair to the people against whom the dilemma is posed. For example, "America: Love It or Leave It." A more subtle example from a student paper: "Since the universe could not have been created out of nothingness, it must have been created by an intelligent life force. . . ." Well, maybe, but is creation by an intelligent life force the *only* other possibility? This argument **overlooks alternatives.**

Ethical arguments seem especially prone to false dilemmas. Either the fetus is a human being with all the rights you and I have, we say, or else it is a lump of tissue with no moral significance at all. Either every use of animal products is wrong, or all of the current uses are acceptable. In fact, other possibilities usually exist. Try to increase the number of options you consider, not narrow them!

loaded language: language that primarily plays on the emotions. It does not make an argument at all, in truth, but is only a form of manipulation. See Rule 5.

mere redescription: Offering a premise that really only rephrases the conclusion, rather than offering a specific, independent reason for it. (**Mere redescription** is a form of **begging the question**, broadly speaking, but here the premise and the conclusion are not distinguished enough for us to say that the premise really presupposes the conclusion. It's more helpful to recognize mere redescription as a separate fallacy.)

> **Leo:** Marisol is a fine architect.
>
> **Laila:** Why do you say that?
>
> **Leo:** Marisol is a very capable designer of buildings.

But being a fine architect is basically the same thing as being a very capable designer of buildings. Leo hasn't really offered any specific evidence for his first claim, but only *restated* it. Actual evidence might be professional recognitions and well-regarded buildings that Marisol has designed.

A classical satirical example of **mere redescription** occurs in Molière's play *The Imaginary Invalid*. One of the stuffed-shirt doctors explains why a certain medicine helps people to sleep by saying that it has a "dormitive principle." This sounds very helpful and scientific until you realize that it simply says that the medicine puts people to sleep—nothing about how or why. It looks like an explanation but in fact it explains nothing, only repeats itself in Latin. Ig-Bay eal-Day.

non sequitur: drawing a conclusion that "does not follow," that is, a conclusion that is not a reasonable inference from, or even related to, the evidence. This is a very general term for a bad argument. Try to figure out specifically what is supposed to be wrong with it.

overgeneralizing: generalizing from too few examples. Just because your student friends are all athletes or business majors or vegetarians, it doesn't follow that *all* of your fellow students are the same (remember Rules 7 and 8). You can't generalize even from a large sample unless it is demonstrably representative. Take care!

overlooking alternatives: forgetting that things may happen for a variety of reasons, not just one. For example, Rule 19 pointed out that just because events E_1 and E_2 may correlate, it does not follow that E_1 causes E_2. E_2 could cause E_1; something else could cause *both* E_1 and E_2; E_1 may cause E_2 *and* E_2 may cause E_1; or E_1 and E_2 might not even be related. **False dilemma** is another example: there are usually many more options than two.

persuasive definition: defining a term in a way that may seem to be straightforward but in fact is loaded. For example, someone might define "evolution" as "the atheistic view that species develop as a result of mere chance events over a supposed period of billions of years." Persuasive definitions may be favorably loaded too: for example, someone might define a "conservative" as "a person with a realistic view of human limits."

petitio principii: Latin for **begging the question**.

poisoning the well: using **loaded language** to disparage an argument before even mentioning it.

> I'm confident you haven't been taken in by those few holdouts who still haven't outgrown the superstition that . . .

More subtly:

> No sensitive person thinks that . . .

post hoc, ergo propter hoc (literally, "after this, therefore because of this"; sometimes just called the *post hoc fallacy*): assuming causation too readily on the basis of mere succession in time. Again a very general term for what Chapter V tries to make precise. Return to Chapter V and try to figure out if other causal explanations are more plausible.

red herring: introducing an irrelevant or secondary subject and thereby diverting attention from the main subject. Usually the red herring is an issue about which people get heated quickly, so that no one notices how their attention is being diverted. In a discussion of the relative safety of different makes of cars, for instance, the issue of which cars are made in America is a red herring.

straw person: a caricature of an opposing view, exaggerated from what anyone is likely to hold, so that it is easy to refute. See Rule 5.

Appendix II

Definitions

Some arguments require attention to the meaning of words. Sometimes we may not know the established meaning of a word, or the established meaning may be specialized. If the conclusion of your argument is that "Wejacks are herbivorous," your first task is to define your terms, unless you are speaking to an Algonquian ecologist.[11] If you encounter this conclusion elsewhere, the first thing you need is a dictionary.

Other times, a term may be in popular use but still unclear. We debate "assisted suicide," for example, but don't necessarily understand exactly what it means. Before we can argue effectively about it, we need an agreed-upon idea of what we are arguing *about*.

Still another kind of definition is required when the meaning of a term is contested. What is a "drug," for example? Is alcohol a drug? Is tobacco? What if they are? Can we find any logical way to answer these questions?

When terms are unclear, get specific

A neighbor of mine was taken to task by the city's Historic Districts Commission for putting up a four-foot model lighthouse in her front yard. City ordinances prohibit any yard fixtures in historic districts. She was hauled before the commission

---

11. "Wejack" is the Algonquian name for a weasel-like animal of eastern North America called the "fisher" in English. "Herbivores" are animals that eat only or mostly plants. Actually, wejacks are not herbivorous.

and told to remove it. A furor erupted and the story got into the newspapers.

Here the dictionary saved the day. According to *Webster's*, a "fixture" is something fixed or attached, as to a building, such as a permanent appendage or structural part. The lighthouse, however, was moveable—more like a lawn ornament. Hence, it was not a "fixture"—seeing as the law did not specify any alternative definition. Hence, not prohibited.

When issues get more difficult, dictionaries are less helpful. Dictionary definitions often offer synonyms, for one thing, that may be just as unclear as the word you're trying to define. Dictionaries also may give multiple definitions, so you have to choose between them. And sometimes, dictionaries are just plain wrong. *Webster's* may be the hero of the last story, but it also defines "headache" as "a pain in the head"—far too broad a definition. A bee sting or cut on your forehead or nose would be a pain in the head but not a headache.

For some words, then, you need to make the term more precise yourself. Use concrete, definite terms rather than vague ones (Rule 4). Be specific without narrowing the term too much.

> Organic foods are foods produced without chemical fertilizers or pesticides.

Definitions like this call a clear idea to mind, something you can investigate or evaluate. Be sure, of course, to stick to your definition as you go on with your argument (no equivocation).

One virtue of the dictionary is that it is fairly neutral. *Webster's* defines "abortion," for example, as "the forcible expulsion of the mammalian fetus prematurely." This is an appropriately neutral definition. It is not up to the dictionary to decide if abortion is moral or immoral. Compare a common definition from one side of the abortion debate:

> "Abortion" means "murdering babies."

This definition is loaded. Fetuses are not the same as babies, and the term "murder" unfairly imputes evil intentions to well-intentioned people. That ending the life of a fetus is comparable to ending the life of a baby is an arguable proposition, but it is for an argument to *show*—not simply *assume* by definition. (See also Rule 5, and the fallacy of persuasive definition.)

You may need to do a little research. You will find, for example, that "assisted suicide" means allowing doctors to help aware and rational people arrange and carry out their own dying. It does not include allowing doctors to "unplug" patients without their consent (that would be some form of "involuntary euthanasia"—a different category). People may have good reasons to object to assisted suicide so defined, but if the definition is made clear at the outset, at least the contending parties will be talking about the same thing.

Sometimes we can define a term by specifying certain tests or procedures that determine whether or not it applies. This is called an *operational* definition. For example, Wisconsin law requires that all legislative meetings be open to the public. But what exactly counts as a "meeting" for purposes of this law? The law offers an elegant criterion:

> A "meeting" is any gathering of enough legislators to block action on the legislative measure that is the subject of the gathering.

This definition is far too narrow to define the ordinary word "meeting." But it does accomplish the purpose of this law: to prevent legislators from making crucial decisions out of the public eye.

When terms are contested, work from the clear cases

Sometimes a term is *contested*. That is, people argue over the proper application of the term itself. In that case, it's not enough simply to propose a clarification. A more involved kind of argument is needed.

When a term is contested, you can distinguish three relevant sets of things. One set includes those things to which the term clearly applies. The second includes those things to which the term clearly does *not* apply. In the middle will be those things whose status is unclear—including the things being argued over. Your job is to formulate a definition that

1. *includes* all the things that the term clearly fits;

2. *excludes* all the things that the term clearly does not fit; and

3. draws the *plainest possible line* somewhere in between, and *explains* why the line belongs there and not somewhere else.

For example, consider what defines a "bird." Exactly what is a bird, anyway? Is a bat a bird?

To meet requirement 1, it is often helpful to begin with the general category (*genus*) to which the things being defined belong. For birds, the natural genus would be animals. To meet requirements 2 and 3, we then need to specify how birds differ from other animals (the *differentia*). Our question therefore is: precisely what differentiates birds—*all* birds and *only* birds—from other animals?

It's trickier than it may seem. We can't draw the line at flight, for example, because ostriches and penguins don't fly (so the proposed definition wouldn't cover all birds, violating the first requirement), and bumblebees and mosquitoes do (so the proposed definition would include some nonbirds, violating the second).

What distinguishes all and only birds, it turns out, is having feathers. Penguins and ostriches have feathers even though they don't fly—they're still birds. But flying insects do not, and neither (in case you were wondering) do bats.

Now consider a harder case: what defines a "drug"?

Start again with the clear cases. Heroin, cocaine, and marijuana clearly are drugs. Air, water, most foods, and shampoos clearly are *not* drugs—though all of these are "substances," like drugs, and are all ingested or applied to our body parts. Unclear cases include tobacco and alcohol.[12]

Our question, then, is: Does any general description cover *all* of the clear cases of drugs and *none* of the substances that clearly aren't drugs, drawing a clear line in between?

A drug has been defined—even by a presidential commission— as a substance that affects mind or body in some way. But this

---

12. Unclear in another way are substances such as aspirin, antibiotics, vitamins, and antidepressants—the kinds of substances we buy in "drugstores" and call "drugs" in a pharmaceutical sense. But these are *medicines* and not drugs in the moral sense we are exploring.

definition is far too broad. It includes air, water, food, and so on, too, so it fails on the second requirement.

We also can't define a drug as an *illegal* substance that affects mind or body in some way. This definition might cover more or less the right set of substances, but it does not meet requirement 3. It does not explain why the line belongs where it is. After all, part of the point of trying to define "drug" in the first place might well be to decide which substances *should* be legal and which should not! Defining a drug as an illegal substance short-circuits this project. (Technically, it commits the fallacy of begging the question.)

Try this:

> A "drug" is a substance used primarily to alter our state of mind in some specific way.

Heroin, cocaine, and marijuana obviously count. Food, air, and water don't—because even though they have effects on the mind, the effects are not specific and are not the primary reason why we eat, breathe, and drink. Unclear cases we then approach with the question: is the *primary* effect *specific* and on the *mind?* Perception-distorting and mood-altering effects do seem to be the chief concern in current moral debates about drugs, so arguably this definition captures the kind of distinction people really want to make.

Should we add that drugs are addictive? Maybe not. Some substances are addictive but not drugs—certain foods, perhaps. And what if a substance that "alter[s] our state of mind in some specific way" turns out to be *non*addictive (as some people have claimed about marijuana, for example)? Is it therefore not a drug? Maybe addiction defines "drug *abuse*," but not "drug" as such.

D3
Definitions don't replace arguments

Definitions help us to organize our thoughts, group like things with like, and pick out key similarities and differences. Sometimes, after words are clearly defined, people may even discover that they do not really disagree about an issue at all.

By themselves, though, definitions seldom settle difficult questions. We seek to define "drug," for example, partly to decide what sort of stance to take toward certain substances. But such a definition cannot answer this question by itself. Under the proposed definition, coffee is a drug. Caffeine certainly alters the state of the mind in specific ways. It is even addictive. But does it follow that coffee should be banned? No, because the effect is mild and socially positive for many people. Some attempt to weigh benefits against harms is necessary before we can draw any conclusions.

Marijuana is a drug under the proposed definition. Should *it* be banned? Just as with coffee, more argument is necessary. Some people claim that marijuana has only mild and socially positive effects too. Supposing they're right, you could argue that marijuana shouldn't be banned even though it is a drug (like coffee). Others argue that it has far worse effects and tends to be a "gateway" to harder drugs besides. If they're right, you could argue for banning marijuana whether it is a drug or not.

Or perhaps marijuana is most akin to certain antidepressants and stimulants—medicines that (take note) also turn out to be drugs on the proposed definition, but call not for bans but for *control*.

Alcohol, meanwhile, is a drug under the proposed definition. In fact, it is the most widely used drug of all. Its harms are enormous, including kidney disease, birth defects, half of all traffic deaths, and more. Should it be limited or banned? Maybe—although there are counterarguments too. Once again, though, this question is not settled by the determination that alcohol is a drug. Here the *effects* make the difference.

In short, definitions contribute to clarity, but seldom do they make arguments all by themselves. Clarify your terms—know exactly what questions you're asking—but don't expect that clarity alone will answer them.

Resources

The general subject of this book is usually labeled "critical thinking." If you're a student wanting to learn more about the subject, look for Critical Thinking courses or other introductory philosophy courses with "reasoning" in their title that are offered at your school. To read more, you can find dozens of textbooks for such courses online or in college or university libraries, including David Morrow's and my *A Workbook for Arguments* (Hackett, Second Edition, 2016), a companion keyed exactly to this book. Another good recent text is Lewis Vaughn's *The Power of Critical Thinking* (Oxford, many editions).

Critical thinking used to be called "informal logic," in contrast to the formal kind. The study of formal logic begins with the deductive forms presented in Chapter VI and expands them into a symbolic system of much greater scope. If you want to look in that direction, once again there are dozens of textbooks and other guides available, under the keywords "logic" or "symbolic logic." Some textbooks combine formal and informal logic: a fine example is David Kelley, *The Art of Reasoning* (Norton, Fourth Edition, 2013).

The field of rhetoric examines the persuasive use of language, especially in arguments. One good text in the field is *The Aims of Argument: A Text and Reader* by Timothy Crusius and Carolyn Channell (McGraw-Hill, many editions). For an "invitational," noncombative approach to rhetoric and oral argumentation, see Sonja and Karen Foss' excellent *Inviting Transformation: Presentational Speaking for a Changing World* (Waveland Press, Third Edition, 2011). A useful guide to the rhetorical as well as logical "moves" in academic writing in particular is Gerald Graff and Cathy Birkenstein's *They Say, I Say* (Norton, Third Edition, 2014).

On the role of critical thinking in ethics, see my book *A 21st Century Ethical Toolbox* (Oxford, Fourth Edition, 2018). On the role of ethics in critical thinking, see Chapters 11 and 12 of *Toolbox*, specifically, as well as Martin Fowler's *The Ethical Practice of Critical Thinking* (Carolina Academic Press, 2008). On the creative writing of arguments, see Frank Cioffi, *Imaginative Argument: A Practical Manifesto for Writers* (Princeton University Press, 2005).

On the fallacies specifically, see Howard Kahane and Nancy Cavendar, *Logic and Contemporary Rhetoric* (Wadsworth, many editions).

On style, still unmatched is William Strunk and E. B. White's *The Elements of Style* (Macmillan, many editions)—a book in spirit much like this one. Keep them together on a shelf somewhere, and don't let them gather dust!